Jean Bovell

From HUMBLE BEGINNINGS

- The *Extraordinary Story* of C.K. Sylvester -

JEAN BOVELL

Published by Dolman Scott Ltd
Copyright Jean Bovell 2016

All rights reserved. No part of this publication may be reproduced, stored in a retrieval system, or transmitted in any form or by any means, electronic, mechanical, photocopy, recording or otherwise, without prior written permission of the copyright owner. Nor can it be circulated in any form of binding or cover other than that in which it is published and without similar condition including this condition being imposed on a subsequent purchaser

ISBN: 978-1-911412-04-5

Dolman Scott Ltd
www.dolmanscott.co.uk

PROLOGUE

Cecil Kenrick Sylvester MBE states that his "life history" has been "a most pleasant one".

FROM HUMBLE BEGINNINGS is the biography of Cecil Kenrick Sylvester MBE, commonly known as C.K.

This true-life story offers insight into the background of the community into which our subject was born in the year 1923, before delivering a detailed account of the curious circumstances that resulted in his conception. This true story tells of a child who was abandoned by his father while he was still in the womb and how, as a consequence, he was raised in abject poverty by his single and unsupported mother, whose only means of providing for her family was hard labouring in fields for menial wages. But this mother envisaged a better future for her child, hoping that he would break the generational cycle of poverty that existed within the community into which she was born and he was being raised. She believed firmly that education was the key that would open the door that should lead, ultimately, to a less arduous lifestyle. And despite the costs of higher education being beyond her reach, she remained tenacious in her sacrifices for achieving the desired goal.

The author delivers a broad-based, illustrative and in-depth account of a life history in which diverse and impactful emotional experiences are empathetically unravelled. This narrative begins in the late 1890s and progresses to chronicle one man's intriguing journey from birth on to childhood and adulthood and into his advancing years.

FROM HUMBLE BEGINNINGS is a compelling and fascinating biopic of Cecil Kenrick Sylvester's protracted but inspirational passage from impoverishment to a life of affluence.

Jean Bovell

From Humble Beginnings has been the aspiration of Peter and Yolande Radix.

ACKNOWLEDGEMENTS

Mr Leo Cromwell

Mr Chasley, Theodore David

Mr James Lewis

Mr Michael Marshall

Mrs Loraine Morgan

Mrs Marsha Newton

Mrs Yolande Radix

Dr Peter Radix

Mrs Susan Skeete

Mrs Maria St Bernard

Ms Venita Sylvester

Mr Phillip Kenrick Sylvester

Mr Cecil Kenrick Sylvester MBE

Historical information accessed from:

The Newsroom

The British Library

London

England

CONTENTS

THE CELEBRATION 1
A RURAL SETTING 7
THE HOUSEKEEPER 13
RETURN TO THE STRAW HOUSE 17
CHILDHOOD EXPERIENCES OF C.K. SYLVESTER 25
THE WORLD OF WORK 39
FREE AT LAST 43
THE TURNING POINT 45
STEPPING STONES 49
THE YOUNG FAMILY 53
DESTINY ROAD 57
LOVE AND LOSS 61
OFFSPRING PERCEPTIONS 67
FLYING WITH INDEPENDENT AGENCIES 71
THE EMPLOYER 79
DEALINGS WITH CUSTOMERS 87
THE HELPING HAND 91
GIVING BACK TO SOCIETY 93
ACCOLADES 97
RETIREMENT 99
MOVING ON AFTER RETIREMENT 103
EPILOGUE 107

FROM HUMBLE BEGINNINGS

The extraordinary true-life story of
Cecil Kenrick Sylvester MBE

THE CELEBRATION

Donned in smart but casual-looking, brightly-coloured shirt and with a beaming smile painted on his face, Cecil Kenrick Sylvester MBE, commonly known as C.K., sat centre stage among close family members and friends in a restaurant that overlooked the ocean. He absorbed the surrounding nature reserve and feasted his eyes on the vast blue waters. They were indeed sublime moments and C.K. could think of nowhere better he would rather be on this special day. Indeed, he had for some time harboured the desire to visit this particular eating venue, reputed for its varied and scrumptious cuisine and overall excellent service. And his wish had been granted on discovering that he was being taken to that very place for a surprise milestone birthday celebration by close friends and family members, including daughter Yolande, better known as "Cutie", son Phillip, Kenrick commonly known as "Ken" and their respective partners. The date was 25th February 2013, C.K.'s 90th birthday. And he was in his element.

C.K. remained the focus of attention as beverages were consumed and humorous interactions and outbursts of spontaneous laughter increased at a pace. Soon, the eagerly-awaited separate choices of menu arrived and for a while the previous gleeful chorus was replaced by sounds of contented munching, interrupted only by intermittent sipping of the finest red or white wine from tall, elegant glasses.

After the food had been eaten and the table cleared, everyone commented on their satisfyingly delicious meal. And C.K.'s sparkling expressions spoke volumes. He was not disappointed. He could not be happier. It had been one of the jolliest birthday celebrations he had so far experienced.

But the "Grand Finale" was yet to come. Suddenly, the party erupted into cheers and applause as a waiter impeccably dressed in white uniform appeared. He carried on a silver tray an iced cake adorned with a single candle, and carefully centred it on the table. A member of the group delivered a short speech and C.K.'s birthday was toasted with glasses of champagne. C.K. was elated. And as he prepared to blow out the single candle on his cake, cries of "Make a wish, make a wish" rang in his ears. He duly obliged, but C.K.'s wish would remain his personal secret. Almost everyone who was also dining at the particular restaurant on the evening of 23rd February 2013 felt compelled to join in with family and friends as they burst merrily into song. And "Happy Birthday to you", closely followed by choruses of "He's a jolly good fellow" that ended with chants of "Hip, hip hoorah", were belted out collectively with considerable gusto and conviction.

"Speech, speech," the group urged. C.K.'s smile broadened and his eyes twinkled as he nodded and sprang to his feet and thanked the intimate little gathering for the most enjoyable birthday surprise. The response was instinctively unanimous as party participants left their seats and warmly embraced or heartily shook hands with the main man of the night. He was truly moved. It had been an evening to remember.

C.K. remained exhilarated during the entire return journey to the home he shared with his younger son Brian. And when eventually he climbed between the sheets of his large and comfortable bed, he glanced at the clock and smiled. Way past the bed-time for an old man, he joked to himself, but reasoned that it was "worth it". He had had a ball! C.K. was unable to relax into sleep as ninety years of life experiences that seemed to have hurried by in an instant, flashed before him. To have actually arrived at this landmark birthday had been a most significant attainment. He had made it! And in self-congratulatory mood he could think of no better way to end the amazing occasion than wallowing for a while in the "good old days". C.K. glowed with mixed feelings of pride and pleasure as he relived only the gloriously unforgettable highpoints of his life thus far.

How could he ever forget the thrill of his very first momentous achievement, and he swelled a little as he recalled being one of only four boys island-wide to have won an annual scholarship for entry into Secondary School. The year was 1935 and C.K. was just 12 years old.

And, of course, the day he married his first love, the beautiful Vernice Banfield, and the flush of happiness that washed over him as they stood together before the priest. And though the blissful memories of love were tinged with sadness, C.K. refused to allow negative thoughts to take hold. He was focused solely on the positives and in particular the arrival of three healthy offspring, namely Yolande, better known as "Cutie", Cecily and Phillip, Kenrick, commonly known as "Ken". Siblings Brian and Sharon resulted from a second marriage, but the birth of each of his five children had been no less uniquely special.

C.K. recollected being gripped by intense feelings of elation when news broke that the Grenadian cricketer Junior Murray had been included in the West Indies Cricket Team. Murray had been the very first local boy to have been selected for the professional team and C.K. was so overwhelmingly "chuffed" that he became the sportsman's biggest supporter and cheerleader. He could not help but smile at the wonderful memory.

On receiving information that he was being honoured with an MBE by Her Majesty, The Queen of England, for his steadfast support and sponsorship of various sporting activities, C.K. was both grateful and humbled. He had always been interested in sport and would have loved to be an active participant, but lacked the necessary agility. C.K. did the next best thing and derived great satisfaction by helping the naturally-gifted to reach their sporting potential.

And how could C.K. ever forget almost exploding with pride on receiving news that his friend Julius Isaac had been appointed Chief Judge in Canada? C.K. assisted Julius when both boys were at school together and continued to tutor the ambitious young man during his time in higher education. Julius went on to study Law in Canada and had now progressed to being the first black lawyer to have attained the prestigious position in the far-away country. It had been a highly-rewarding moment for C.K.

The interlude of rewinding and reliving congratulatory moments may have been a rare occurrence for a man who had not been known to blow his own trumpet. But at aged 90, he should have earned the right to wallow a little in past glory.

Now in his twilight years, C.K. was enjoying good health and fitness. He was still independently competent at the wheel of his Range Rover and enjoyed invigorating morning swims at nearby Lans Aux Epines beach. His love of sport, particularly cricket, had not diminished and he never missed a game. Always a practising Catholic, C.K. in retirement devoted more time to his religion. He supported the local church choir and accompanied them on trips abroad. C.K. also kept a hand in the business he founded by now and again dropping into his old offices. The overall quality of life for this particular old-timer was undeniably very good. He was, at 90, very much a contented soul.

With a smile still lingering on his face, C.K. drifted into deep and satisfying slumber. Apart from being blessed with the gifts that cannot be purchased with money, never in his wildest dreams would he have imagined the magnitude of his success in a career that was not planned or even aspired to. He may have been steered by destiny onto a fortuitous path; but there could be no doubt that C.K. Sylvester had been dealt an extraordinary hand.

A RURAL SETTING

Sylvester had been a well-known family name on the island of Grenada, with branches in various areas across the land. A number of individuals who carried the surname Sylvester were politicians, entrepreneurs, others were highly-respected educators, particularly so in the Parish of St David. But there were also branches of the Sylvester clan who struggled on the poverty line.

Albertha Sylvester had been a product of poverty-stricken relations. She was born in the 1890s and raised in a small but supportive settlement community where everyone carried the surname "Sylvester". The settlement was located within the village of Morne Delice in an area of St Paul's known as The Mang.

The village of Morne Delice was at the time densely populated with trees. The terrain consisted of pathways that were hazardously uneven and muddy, and particularly slippery on rainy days. The residents of Morne Delice lived in "straw houses". These basic dwellings were structured with wood that had been extracted from discarded boxes and large quantities of straw were used for covering-up the many gaps and protecting against outside elements. The majority of straw houses contained very little furniture and would be at best basic, such as a single bed and a table and a few chairs that had been crudely assembled with wood taken from trees or boxes. Meals were prepared on outdoor log fires. Latrines were enclosed dug-out holes and water was accessed from a nearby stream.

The adults who lived in the village were employed as unskilled labourers or hired to work the land on various estates across the parishes. The only free education available was primary and delivered to children at the local Elementary school until they reached the age of 14.

Many in the community owned just one decent outfit which was mainly reserved for Church on Sunday. Garments worn on a day-to-day basis were shabby or ripped and villagers walked long distances in bare feet. Only the very few owned shoes or were able to obtain rides on the backs of horses or even donkeys. These animals, owned mainly by the better-off in the society of the day, had been the known alternative source of transport. And the vast majority of ordinary folk simply moved around on toughened bare feet that were adept in tackling unpredictable and perilous terrains.

Despite the material deprivation, it had been an accepted way of life. And underpinned by their unshakeable Christian Faith, always a source of solace, this settlement of poverty-stricken Sylvesters were contently unified in their strong sense of family and belonging. The children played and there were many moments of fun, laughter and impromptu celebrations. Occasions such as Christmas, Christenings and weddings were enthusiastically organised and highly enjoyable events.

Like many other young people from the area, Albertha sought employment on the estates after leaving school. Those who were fortunate in finding "work" as maids or gardeners at the homes of those who were relatively well-off were considered "lucky". But unskilled workers in those days were very much exploited and monthly salaries were minimal.

World War I had ended. The year was 1918 and Albertha Sylvester had been a labouring hand on an estate for a number of years when it was one day announced that a new "Over-Seer from England" had taken over and would someday soon visit the estate. Everyone, including Albertha, was curious and eager to "see what this Englishman looked like".

The particular Englishman was called Percy Henderson and he had arrived on the island with the responsibility of managing the British-owned Grenada-based firm Hubbard and Company Limited and also various British-owned estates on the island.

When the day of the expected visit arrived, all workers kept their heads down and in silence focused on specific tasks as Percy Henderson, with the Estate Supervisor by his side, carried out the required inspections.

No one was aware that Henderson had observed a particularly pretty young worker who appeared healthy and wholesome and generally pleasing to the eye. Henderson had been for some time on the look-out for a suitable housekeeper and this young lady, in his view, seemed a suitable candidate for the vacant position. Percy wasted no time speaking to the Supervisor of the Estate in relation to arranging an interview on his behalf with Albertha Sylvester at Henderson's house on a specified day the following week.

Albertha was visibly stunned and shaken on being informed of the proposed job interview. It was totally unexpected and a bolt out of the blue. Relatives in the village were equally surprised when Albertha told them of the unexpected opportunity that had come her way. And it was not long before the entire village was buzzing with the exciting news that one of their own would soon be keeping house for a "Big Shot from England!" It was almost like winning the Sweep Stake which was, in those days, equivalent to winning the National Lottery.

On the day of the arranged meeting, Albertha awoke at the crack of dawn and went down to the river, where she bathed and washed her hair. After breakfast, she greased and fixed her hair neatly and attractively. She then put on her best blue dress and her one and only pair of cheap canvas shoes and offered up a prayer before setting off on the journey to Percy Henderson's residence in a comparatively affluent neighbourhood in St Paul's.

On arrival, Albertha was immediately drawn to the vehicle that was parked at the front of the house. Only the "wealthy" on the island owned motor cars in those days and it was, as a consequence, indicative of Henderson's privileged status. And it was with this fact in mind that Albertha was nervously hesitant as she knocked gently on the door of Percy Henderson's house. But she was surprisingly taken aback by the friendly greeting she received from her seemingly "down-to-earth" prospective employer.

"Come on in," Henderson said cheerfully, "and do take a seat."

"Thank you," replied Albertha before easing carefully down at the end of a cushioned chair while at the same time casting her eyes around the airy and classically furnished "drawing room". It was a far cry from anything she had ever seen before. Albertha wondered whether she was really a visitor at the home of the distinguished-looking Percy Henderson or had been "caught up" in a dream from which she would at any minute wake up. But she was jolted into stark reality when Percy asked if she was capable of maintaining a house, prepare meals and undertake laundering tasks that would include ironing and mending or altering garments whenever necessary. Albertha had experienced carrying out all of the required tasks and her reply was an enthusiastic "yes".

Percy in return did not hesitate in offering the young woman the position of live-in housekeeper at his home at a salary that was well above what she had ever previously received. Albertha had no control over the high-pitched excited tones in which she gushed her "thank you" response to her soon-to-be employer.

At the end of the interview, Percy Henderson shook the hand of Albertha and with a smile bade her goodbye. Overcome with feelings of delight, Albertha once again expressed heartfelt gratitude to Henderson, before embarking on the return journey to her home village. "What a nice man," she told herself. She could hardly believe that the English gentleman had actually shaken her hand. And twice at that! This was during a period when the class divide had been rigidly adhered to and people in authority were highly respected. Albertha was thrilled to bits and over the moon. She felt as though she had just been handed a passport to a better life and with clenched fist she punched the air victoriously at the thought of no longer having to work in the fields under the heat of the sun for only a few shillings at the end of each month. Thank you, Lord, she cried out loudly as she rushed to spread the news of her newly-secured work position to relatives back in the village.

Needless to say, the community as a whole was deliriously happy and proud of Albertha's "stroke of good luck" and one by one embraced and wished her the very best.

Two weeks later and carrying a bag that had been made from cloth which contained her few belongings, Albertha said good-bye to relatives as they stood outside their humble straw houses with huge smiles on their faces and waved wildly and spontaneously. Albertha promised to visit them on her free days. It had been a memorable moment in time.

THE HOUSEKEEPER

Percy Henderson opened the door of his home to Albertha Sylvester as she arrived to begin her duties as housekeeper. She was happy and filled with optimism. The day promised a new dawn into a brighter future. The thought that destiny's plan may, further down the line, steer her along an altogether different path had not even entered her head.

After being guided around the house and shown her living quarters, Henderson proceeded to inform Albertha of the various tasks required that day. He then jumped into and noisily revved up the engine of his quaint little vehicle and drove to his office at Hubbard & Co. The management of the day-to-day upkeep of his home was left in what he hoped would be the capable hands of Albertha.

Albertha was anxious and eager to please. She was determined to work hard and prove to Henderson that she was a very good housekeeper. She tied her hair with a scarf, slipped on an apron, grabbed a broom and was ready to go, and hummed and sang joyfully as she carried out the various chores. It was a wonderful feeling of freedom to be working in a pleasant environment with no one "breathing down her neck". And she was in her element to be in control of her domain during the period her employer was at his office. Albertha could not help but gleefully break into dance as she skipped from one task to the next, all the while being mindful that every chore undertaken should be completed to the best of her ability.

Henderson returned from work that very afternoon to a meal that was ready and waiting on the table and a house that was spick and span. He was duly impressed. And when being complimented by her employer after he had in no time at all "polished off" every morsel of food on the dish, Albertha shyly placed a hand over her mouth and giggled with delight. She had on the very first day succeeded in proving her capabilities and could not have been more pleased with herself.

The following morning, Albertha again began her household duties by preparing breakfast for her employer and continued with the remaining required tasks following his departure for work. The daily routines remained unchanged except for Sunday. After being served an early breakfast on the day of rest, Henderson would get into his motor vehicle and drive himself to the Anglican Church in time for the Sunday Service. He would afterwards spend the rest of the day visiting with friends.

Albertha, on the other hand, would walk at a leisurely pace to the Catholic Church where she attended Mass. Sunday was her free day and when the ceremony was over, she would head towards her home village. The various family members were always pleased to see her and regularly commented on how well she looked. Albertha appeared increasingly "chunky" since starting her new job and in an era when "roly-poly" signified wellness and fitness, everyone was assured that she had found her feet and was now "living the life".

Following a relaxed day spent in her home village, Albertha would embark on the return journey to Henderson's house before the onset of dusk. There were no street lights in the area of the period and she was mindful of the risks involved in walking unaccompanied in the pitch black of night. During the journey her mind would linger on Henderson and in particular she wondered whether or not he would be climbing into her bed "tonight".

Albertha had not been long in the job when Henderson made advances towards her. It became apparent that she was not just taken on as housekeeper but was also required to fulfil her employer's lustful desires. The housekeeper felt powerless and even embarrassingly intimidated, but certainly lacked the assertiveness required to question her employer's motives. She was, after all, really only the maid and not only did she need the job but it was also the best she had ever had. And so it was, without protest, Albertha yielded to Henderson's personal demands. But she may have been at the time a simple soul and naive to the probability of being somewhat exploited having fitted the bill for the twin role of housekeeper as well as bed-mate.

Time marched on and within the Henderson household daily housekeeping routines were very often followed by nightly frolics between the sheets, but consequences may not have been considered. And when, in the year 1922, Albertha began to experience symptoms indicating that she may be pregnant, her life seemed to have been turned upside down. She had no idea where to turn and felt tongue-tied in broaching the subject with Henderson. There had never been any lengthy or meaningful conversation between employer and employee. Henderson spoke to his housekeeper only on matters related to work requirements or when he thanked her for meals that had been exceptionally enjoyed. He may also from time to time praise her laundering skills, particularly with regard to his perfectly-ironed bleached white shirts. And although Albertha's responses may have been appropriate in context, they were more than likely limited to a one-syllable "Yes", "No", "Thanks", or a smile that mirrored gratitude.

But the previously contented housemaid was now at a worrisome stage. Her usual gleeful demeanour was no more and she concentrated on praying for guidance on the best way forward. It was, nonetheless, inevitable that her condition would at some point come to light and the day eventually arrived when Henderson expressed the suspicion that she was with child. Albertha was relieved that, after months of anxiety and apprehension, she was at last being enabled to reveal directly to the man who asked the question that she was indeed expecting his baby. The feeling of relief that came with being at long last enabled to share the previously concealed life-altering information with the significant other person had been immeasurable.

Life in the Henderson household continued as normal, but the air had been cleared and resulted in routine housekeeping requirements being undertaken in a happier frame of mind. This situation was, however, short-lived, as not long before the baby was expected to arrive, Henderson announced that he had been feeling unwell and needed to go to England to have his condition investigated. The housekeeper was assured by her employer that she would be expected to resume working for him after his return to the island. He would also have no objection to the expected child's presence at the house. Albertha was thrilled and dared to imagine cosy domesticity with Henderson and their new baby. After months of frantic uncertainty, everything in the garden was now appearing rosy and not a dark cloud was to be spotted hovering on the horizon.

RETURN TO THE STRAW HOUSE

Albertha was warmly welcomed on arrival at her home village, but word had been passed around that she was back for a short while only and would soon be returning to her housekeeping tasks at the house of Percy Henderson. And news regarding her pregnancy had already been spread like wildfire across the village. In those days children were considered "little blessings" sent by God to maintain the upkeep of the community and safeguard the welfare of elders in their dotage. Albertha was, in particular, considered most fortunate to have been impregnated by a "wealthy" Englishman who would undoubtedly prove to be a most generous provider. Relatives in the village of Morne Delice were proud and happy that their girl had done so well.

The eagerness and impatience experienced by Albertha coming up to the birth of her child had been two-fold. Not only was she anxious for indicators that delivery was imminent, but she was also caught up in continuing feelings of anticipation. She looked forward excitedly to the day when once again she would leave the family's straw house and, proudly carrying her new baby, return to housekeeping duties at the home of the father of her child. Albertha did not doubt for a single moment that Henderson would keep his promise. She could hardly wait for the happy day to arrive, but time seemed to be dragging so slowly.

New Year is universally a time for celebration and renewed hope for the future. And so it was on the eve of the dawning of 1923 on the island of Grenada. It was a time of festivity and goodwill with "Happy New Year" sentiments being reciprocally extended. Personal wishes and intentions were expressed, but essentially everyone hoped for better during the course of the year ahead. In the particular case of Albertha, the safe delivery of a healthy and well-formed baby had been the priority consideration.

The 1920s was a modern age of fresh and liberated attitudes following World War I. It was a time when motor vehicles ruled the roads. And young women discarded previously-worn long skirts and hair, and replaced them with knee-length dresses accessorised with long-hanging beads, and styled haircuts. New music, namely Jazz and Blues, was being introduced and exported throughout the Western world by the United States. And even though prohibition – a ban on alcohol – had been enforced, it was nonetheless a "good time" era, known historically as the Roaring Twenties or the Jazz Age. A decade when youth ruled and the effervescent new generation otherwise known as "The bright young things", dressed in trendy outfits of the day and gleefully danced "The Charleston" by swinging their arms while stepping backwards, forwards and sideways in time to the rhythms played out by live jazz bands.

Although the dominant music and dance culture had spilled over into the Caribbean islands, Grenada was among English-speaking British colonies in the region that maintained, in various aspects, a way of life that mirrored the Colonial Power. It included children being taught English history in every school. In particular, the Secondary schools' curriculum reflected those of the British, including the Cambridge-set final examinations; vehicles were driven on the left side of the road; and the currency was pound sterling.

Among events that occurred in Great Britain during the year 1923, none was more significant than the marriage between the then Prince Albert, Duke of York, and Lady Elizabeth Bowes-Lyon. The Royal couple were in 1937 crowned King George VI and Queen Elizabeth following the abdication of his elder brother, King Edward VIII in 1936. The new King and Queen were the parents of the present Queen, Elizabeth II.

Specifically on the island of Grenada, 1923 saw the establishment of seven additional Police Stations. It resulted in the number of Police Officers being increased to 92. And a new Chief of Police was appointed.

The island's General Hospital, located in the city of George, was initially designed to provide services to the British Military, but in 1864 had been handed over to the people. The transition required appropriate remodelling and expansion suitable to serving the varied and complex needs of the general population and was carried out in stages over subsequent years.

Albertha was admitted to the renovated General Hospital, known also as the Colony Hospital, in February 1923 to await delivery of the expected child. After many hours of agonising pain, the moment eventually arrived when Albertha was overcome by an "almighty" urge to push. And within seconds a well-formed infant, at considerable speed, gushed into the world and was instantaneously caught by the attending midwife.

"Congratulations, it's a boy!" she exclaimed. And as the oxygen of life filled his tiny lungs, everyone was assured by the gutsy cries that the new-born child was alive and healthy. The date was Friday 23rd February 1923.

The exhausted first-time mother glowed with pride and happiness as the little one was for the first time placed in her arms and she marvelled at how the previously-endured excruciating pain had so suddenly vanished. Albertha would decide then and there that her baby boy would continue the paternal lineage by carrying the surname of his father. If only "Mr Henderson" was here to see his beautiful new-born son, she sighed.

The community of Morne Delice had been supportive and willing to provide assistance to separate family units and in particular single-parent households. But this particular first-time mother and child were not expected to remain members of the community for too much longer. Albertha had boasted of the mutual agreement with her employer and that she would resume her live-in position on his return. And, moreover, she would be accompanied by their child.

It was with this conviction at the forefront of her mind that the infant was baptised in the Anglican Church and given the name Ralph Henderson. Although the chosen religion was taken against the expectations of Roman Catholic relatives, the priority at that time was meeting the approval of Percy Henderson, who was known to be a practising member of the Church of England. The child was as a consequence baptised into the Anglican religion.

Albertha imagined Mr Henderson's approval on learning that their son not only shared his name but, equally importantly, his Faith. Despite being herself a devoted Catholic, she felt sure that her single-minded decisions would serve the best interests of their son.

Albertha held fast to the belief that Henderson would someday come home, even though time was passing by and he was yet to make an appearance. All the while, little Ralph was growing and developing into a bright and precocious toddler. And it was at this point that the young mother began to think of his schooling. She knew well that young inquisitive brains were receptive to learning and retaining information and that having access to a sound educational foundation could be advantageous to her son's school career. With those factors in mind, Ralph was enrolled into the best preparatory fee-paying school available in the area and Albertha returned to working on the Estate to earn the money needed for paying the required fees. This was considered a temporary solution pending Mr Henderson's return, but she believed that the action taken for ensuring that the child's educational interests were being served would undoubtedly receive the approval of his father.

Ralph Henderson had been the only child from the village of Morne Delice who was known to have attended a Prep School and this resulted in a buzz of embellished rumour and whisperings. A relative who to this day continues to reside in the village of Morne Delice, recalled a rumour being bandied around that Albertha denied herself food and ate only the flesh of coconuts to ensure that nearly every penny earned went towards paying the fee for the "little" boy's preparatory education.

And so it was, with a privileged head start, that Ralph Henderson joined other children from poverty-stricken family backgrounds at the local Elementary school. It had also been the point at which Ralph was re-baptised into the Roman Catholic Faith and re-named. The life-changing decision reflected his mother's family name and religious beliefs. After many years of hoping and waiting for Henderson's promised return, Albertha woke up one morning and faced up to the reality that the family had been abandoned and that "Mr Henderson" had no intention of being in the equation. It seemed that while she was looking forward to cosy domesticity with him and the child they made together, he had fled from it. This realisation was compounded by the fact that Mr Henderson left no contact details and had at no time revealed any information regarding his family background.

The harboured sentiments of hope were replaced with a devastating sense of loss, followed by seething anger and the determination to drag herself up from the floor and carry on with her life. Albertha may have questioned why the child should continue to carry the family name of the absent father or even follow his religion. And as a consequence, the first action taken in her quest for a new beginning may well have been the re-baptism and re-naming of her son.

Despite the crushingly disappointing twist of fate that denied her the envisaged comfortable lifestyle at the home of Percy Henderson, Albertha became resigned to being back on "square one", residing in a straw house and working on the Estate. But she was heartened by the presence of a bright and beautiful "little man" in her life. The child had given her a renewed sense of purpose and it was with determination that Albertha slammed the door on personal aspirations and vowed that from "now on" she would not only be his mother, she would also take on the fathering role. Her son and his needs became her priority focus, but in the absence of financial support, she would have to continue working on the Estate to make sure that her "precious boy" was raised to the best of her ability. And apart from the basic requirements of ensuring that he was being well fed, kept clean, adequately clothed and respectful of others, his spiritual and academic education would also be of crucial importance.

In her time, Albertha, like other disadvantaged children who lived in the village of Morne Delice, attended the local Elementary school where she learnt the basics in reading, writing and arithmetic. Higher educational opportunities had been inaccessible. And these children developed into adults with no more expectation than following in the footsteps of their forebears by being the providers of low-paid menial labour to the financially privileged. It was a repeated generational pattern that had become the accepted norm.

Albertha was described as being a sturdily-built woman who always dressed in blue. She had never been seen in any other colour and, as a consequence, was nicknamed "Blue Parrot". She was known also to be a private individual with a serious albeit pleasant persona and altogether a little different in character compared with the majority of women who lived in the village of the day. It was alleged that, following her experiences with Percy Henderson, Albertha became very much self-contained. She rarely mixed, kept herself to herself and refused to engage in the usual female tittle-tattle. And she was, furthermore, reported to have kept far away from other workers on the Estate and would be observed sitting in an isolated area lunching on coconuts while everyone else tucked into previously-prepared wholesome and tasty meals that had been brought from home. It was generally believed that Albertha denied herself for the sake of her son and that almost every penny earned was one way or the other spent on her only son.

Albertha's character had been strengthened following the life-changing events that resulted from her association with Percy Henderson. She was no longer the fanciful and naive little girl and had changed into a strong-minded woman with a purpose. And even though she was trapped in an existence of poverty, Albertha held her head down and refused to be side-tracked from her focus on doing whatever was necessary for enabling a better future for her only son. She was determined that he would break what seemed to be a never-ending circle of poverty and she believed that education was the key; but prayed that destiny would be kind to her boy.

The new beginning as a single unsupported mother began with the re-baptism of little Ralph into the Roman Catholic Faith, under the brand new name of Cecil Kenrick Sylvester. He had been initially Christened in the Anglican Church and named Ralph Henderson. The issued documented proof of the significant conversions brought in its wake a new dawn and the beginning of the life journey of the boy who would thereafter be officially called Cecil Kenrick Sylvester, or commonly C.K.; although various family members and friends continued to call him "Ralph", the name by which they were already familiar.

CHILDHOOD EXPERIENCES OF C.K. SYLVESTER

C.K. crossed the river and hurried barefooted along rugged and muddy pathways with his peers, also in bare feet, to the local Elementary school. The youngsters were eager and anxious to arrive before the bell sounded signalling the start of the school day. As the school house came into view, the boys would race competitively to the finishing line, which in reality were the school's open doors. And just after taking their rightful places, a deafening ringing of bells would reverberate throughout the school house, accompanied by silent sighs of relief. It had been another victorious start for the schoolboys of Morne Delice. They had once again, in the nick of time, beaten the bell and avoided a few sharp lashes from their teacher for being late. Nonetheless, the thrill of the risk was at all times very much worth it!

Despite having the advantage of a private Preparatory education, C.K. was very much accepted as one of the boys. But he harboured a secret which potentially could also have set him apart from his peers in the village. C.K. owned shoes and they did not. Every morning before leaving for school, Albertha would ensure that C.K. wore the pair of shoes she had proudly purchased for him. She had worked hard and scrimped and saved for the required funds. C.K., on the other hand, had other ideas. He had, from a tender age, been empathically aware of the poverty-stricken environment in which he lived. And C.K. did not want to be seen as being different or openly better off in any way. He desired only to be fully integrated as one of the boys. With that endeavour in mind, C.K. contrived a plan. After leaving the family home he would sneak into bushes, remove his shoes and hide them beneath fallen branches. He would then step out in bare feet and join with his barefooted counterparts on the boisterous jaunt to the school house. C.K's little secret was never uncovered.

Despite being prone to having infrequent asthma attacks, C.K. was a basically healthy child who, like the majority of boys, was always a keen participant in adventurous play activities. He was also involved in constructing colourful kites that were flown competitively with kites that were similarly made by other boys in the village during the Easter holiday period. But taking part in sport of any kind had been C.K's favourite activity and although he admits to not being very good at it, cricket was his absolute passion. He would retain a keen interest in sport throughout his life.

Childhood family experiences included memorable fun days when mother and son picnicked on sandy beaches alongside other families. There were also enjoyable visits to friends and relatives who resided in the parish of St David. In particular, C.K. regularly spent a couple of days during the school holidays at the home of his two older "half-sisters" who lived with their mother in a village known as Thebiade, also located in St David's.

At some point during C.K's "growing up years", Albertha discovered by word of mouth that a local woman by the name of Ella James had been in the past employed at the home of an Englishman. This particular gentleman was called Percy Henderson and he resided in the Parish of St David during the first decade of the twentieth century. Ella James and Percy Henderson together produced two daughters named Dreda and Marie Clyne who were born in 1902 and 1905 respectively. The sisters had no recollection of their biological father as he was said to have returned to the U.K. when they were toddlers. But unbeknown to the family Percy Henderson had resurfaced in the Parish of St George many years later.

Maria St Bernard, daughter of Dreda Clyne confirmed that after coming to live in the United Kingdom, the surname "Clyne" was "looked into" by her family and it was determined that "Clyne" was an English family name. Maria added that housemaids being impregnated by British Employers had not been uncommon occurrences in those far gone days.

No one doubted that Dreda and Marie Clyne shared the same biological father with C.K. Sylvester. The siblings were conscious of their mixed race parentage and identified with each other. As a consequence, C.K. was wholeheartedly accepted by his half-sisters as their little brother. He was invited to visit with them during the school holidays and often stayed over for a night or two. Young C.K. was said to be a quiet and well behaved child. And his presence was at all times welcomed at the family home.

C.K.'s mixed background had been a factor that also set him apart from other children in the village. But the personal consequences associated with not having a father in his life could have impacted significantly on the youngster's sense of self. He may have wondered if Percy Henderson ever thought about him. But he had at no time been shown an image of the man who fathered him and whose features, characteristics or even mannerisms he may or may not have inherited. And though he was told of the circumstances surrounding his birth, C.K. had no knowledge of Percy Henderson's actual persona. The questions that remained unanswered in relation to the absent parent resulted in the void that may well have impacted a rounded sense of identity; and, as a consequence, a haunting or enduring emotional aching associated with the "not knowing".

Apart from the academic achievement Albertha aspired for her son, his spiritual education was also crucially important. Albertha engaged her son in reading passages from the Holy Bible and mother and son routinely kneeled together in prayer on waking each day and again before retiring for bed at night. Church attendance on Sunday was "a must" and C.K., along with other children, attended Sunday school where they received doctrine appropriate for taking their First Communion and subsequently the Sacrament of Confirmation. Albertha beamed with pride when her boy was among those selected for the role of Acolyte by the Parish Priest. But even though C.K. had been committed in his role as attendant to the Priest, this fact may not have prevented him joining with other Acolytes, who were at heart mischievous little boys, as they yielded to temptation and helped themselves to a "swig" of the stored Sacred wine before the Holy Chalice was in coy and in pious manner presented to the priest. Nonetheless, the childhood religious experiences would form the basis for his lifelong unwavering Faith.

C.K.'s progress at the public Elementary school had been exceptional. But all the while Albertha was labouring on the Estate, living frugally and making sure that the largest percentage of her hard-earned meagre income was being put aside for purchasing learning tools such as books and writing materials, necessary for promoting her son's education.

Even at just five or six years old, C.K. was well aware that the educational privileges bestowed by his mother that singled him out from his classmates had been a hard-earned priority. In reality, C.K. was no better off than the other children who lived in the village of Morne Delice of the era. Everyone shared the same day-to-day survival struggles. But he was by nature a considerate and helpful child, was sensitively aware of the educational needs of his failing classmates and would often assist them with reading, writing or arithmetic. He was also at all times willing to share his school books with others. The desire to assist others was a characteristic trait that would be carried by C.K. for the rest of his life.

Meanwhile, Albertha remained firm in her endeavour to do everything in her power to ensure a better future for her only son. And so it was that, at the age of nine, C.K. was removed from the local Elementary school and placed into a Catholic Boys' School in the town. The single unsupported mother had been keenly aware of the school's high standards and was confident that the teaching delivered would enable her boy to reach his true potential. It was also an important factor that the particular school was a learning environment that reflected and supported the Religious Faith into which C.K. had been re-baptised. But Albertha's decision, taken in the best interests of her son, resulted in the youngster being somewhat self-conscious in the knowledge that he was once again being singled out by being the only child among his peers in the village whose schooling would progress beyond the basic level. But C.K. had been proved to be a capable young student who was interested in learning new concepts. He was well aware that he was not being fully stretched at the Elementary school he attended.

The new school, J.W. Fletcher, but better known as "Fletcher School", was situated in the city of St George, three miles from the village of Morne Delice. C.K. had no option but to undertake the relatively long walk in his brand-new pair of shoes, but was initially apprehensive about embarking on the journey unaccompanied. There was no need for worrying, as not too far into the walk C.K. encountered various groups of

FROM HUMBLE BEGINNINGS

children along the way who were on a similar journey. And they were all eager to extend a hand of friendship to him. Among the young school travellers were two boys who lived in villages that were close in proximity to Morne Delice.

It was not long before C.K. and his new acquaintances, namely Chasley David and Johnnie Bullen, found that they had a lot in common and firm friendships were developed. The three pals would meet up on school days and accompany each other on the six-mile return journey to and from school. The lads looked forward with enthusiasm to their daily trek, which was always filled with high-jinxed escapades and laughter, fuelled by youthful energy and exuberance. Nonetheless, the boys never failed to arrive at school on time, although they had no idea of specifics in relation to the actual time of day. None of them carried a wrist watch, which in those days was an unaffordable luxury item worn only by the offspring of the "very wealthy".

A member of the friendship trio, Chasley David, recalled the experiences of their daily journey to and from school back in the early 1930s. The boys received no more than a single penny in pocket money from their parents each day. It was a sum that was at the time insufficient for paying the required bus fare, so the boys chose to spend their limited funds on sweets or snacks. Chasley laughed as he explained that despite their impoverished circumstances the buddies very much enjoyed the times they spent together. He recalled their sense of freedom, hilarious banter, playful scuffles and overall youthful exuberance. As the memories came flooding back, Chasley's face lit up and his impish expressions matched the boyish mischievous grin that was reflective of a man reliving his youthful days. He also suggested that there were particular shared experiences he just could not or would not reveal. Nonetheless, there was no denying that for the three buddies, those were indeed "the glory days".

The boys, who were just one or maybe two months apart in age, called each other by nicknames and outside of school would compete against each other in sporting activities such as cricket and football. Despite the pals' youthful jaunts, Chasley, who was in those days known as "Zorro", described the young C.K. as being fundamentally "nice and quiet" and also very bright, possibly the smartest kid at Fletcher School during the period. But he was no "big head". On the contrary, his friend was a humble lad who regularly provided assistance to struggling pupils.

Chasley David, C.K. Sylvester and Johnnie Bullen have remained lifelong friends.

C.K. maintained an excellent record during his attendance at Fletcher School. He achieved a first in each of his subjects and his School Reports contained high praises from his teachers. Needless to say, Albertha was overjoyed. C.K. was her life. She had made so many sacrifices to ensure the necessary funds for purchasing the books required for promoting his education. Her investment had begun to pay dividends and she was happy. C.K. had so far not let her down, but she hoped and prayed that he would continue to excel.

C.K. was 12 years old and had been attending "Fletcher School" for three years when he was rewarded for consistently producing exceptional work. He became the only student at Fletcher School selected to take the National Scholarship Examination for entry into the Grenada Boys' Secondary School in the year 1935. The GBSS was, in those days, a renowned fee-paying educational institution attended mainly by the sons of the relatively better off. On being informed that C.K. had been chosen to sit the annual scholarship examination for entry into the highest school in the land, Albertha was overwhelmed. Of all the pupils attending Fletcher School, her son had been the one picked? She could hardly believe it! The boy had done her so very proud.

It had been Albertha's deeply-held wish that her son would one day become a pupil at the GBSS, but in reality she knew that the required school fees had been far beyond her reach. It seemed an impossible dream. But here she was, repeatedly making thankful Signs of the Cross while struggling to contain the excitement that consumed her. "Imagine that!" she may have told herself. It now appeared that the impossible dream was on the way to becoming an actuality. Albertha only regained her grip when she became mindful of the crucial hurdle that was yet to be cleared. C.K. would have to secure an examination pass before entry into the prestigious academy could be guaranteed. Albertha vowed to provide the material support required for enabling his studies, and, of course, would "pray hard" and remain cautiously optimistic. In the meantime, the family decided to keep their good news a secret from relatives and friends pending the final outcome.

Religious Faith had been fundamental to the family's lifestyle. Mother and son maintained their routine of daily prayer at home and weekly Church attendance. C.K. continued in his role as Acolyte to the Priest during Sunday Mass and he attended a Catholic Boys' School in which prayer and religious studies were incorporated into the curriculum. The experienced religious upbringing resulted in C.K. being, throughout his life, fundamentally a man of God, who endeavoured to live a Christian life.

C.K. studied conscientiously in preparation for taking the Scholarship Examinations, but received additional help and support from his teachers. It was in their interests also that C.K.'s scholarship examination results should reflect correctly the high standards of teaching that were being delivered at Fletcher School. Albertha, as always, ensured that her son possessed the required educational tools and prayed for his success.

On the day the anticipated Scholarship Examinations were scheduled to commence, mother and son were consumed with nervousness, even though the focus remained on the challenge ahead. Albertha wished C.K. well. "Just do your best, son," she assured him. He did indeed knuckle down and produced his best work throughout the examination process, but breathed a deep sigh of relief when the set papers had been fully completed. The subsequent wait for the results would prove to be an anxious and seemingly never-ending period of time.

When the examination results eventually arrived, the news could not have been better. Of the four boys, island-wide, who successfully obtained Scholarships in the year 1935, C.K. was placed second in the overall examination results. There was now no reason for withholding her emotions. Albertha felt immensely gratified and could have burst with pride and joy. C.K. was himself elated. He could hardly believe that he had done so well. The family offered prayers of thanksgiving before revealing their exceptional goods news. The village erupted with euphoria; it had been the first time one of their own had won a Scholarship to attend the prestigious GBSS. It was, for the people of Morne Delice, a phenomenal accomplishment.

Many of the people who lived within the disadvantaged community of the era accepted their lot in life. They had been well aware of their status at the bottom of the ladder and being considered worthy only of carrying out menial jobs that were so under-paid, they could barely afford to adequately feed and clothe their children. Despite that fact, Albertha remained resolute in her aspiration for a better future for her only child. Moreover, the chances of the long-term goal being realised had been bolstered by C.K.'s personal motivations and exceptional academic record, which also served to increase the incentive to carry on the mission. Albertha was now not only overjoyed but believed herself truly blessed to have produced, in her mind, such an intelligent child.

For many, C.K.'s success in obtaining a coveted place at the highest Secondary School of the day had been proof of his academic capacity. But Albertha remained mindful of the fact that her job was not yet done and braced herself for many more years of labouring on the Estate. She had no choice. Where else would the money come from for financially supporting her son's education? Even though Scholarship Award guaranteed free entry into higher education, Albertha was responsible for supplying necessities such as school uniforms, shoes and learning implements such as reading texts, notebooks and implements like pens, pencils, rulers and rubbers.

And so it was, at the beginning of the school year following his Scholarship attainment, young C.K. embarked on his first day's attendance at the Grenada Boys' Secondary School. And in his smart new uniform with its distinguished-looking tie and matching badge, C.K. may have felt himself being transformed into a person of importance befitting of the outfit, such as a young officer or a soldier, even. All the while, many members of their small community stood at their front doors or peered out of windows and wished him well. At the same time, Albertha, with a heart swelled with pride, watched as her son disappeared into the distance. It was for Albertha and also the community an unforgettable day.

But reality would kick-in for C.K. while uncomfortably carrying his heavy books on the three-mile walk to his destination. Winning a Scholarship did not alter the fact that the family's financially disadvantaged status meant that C.K. received just one penny each day from his mother, and it remained his decision whether it was spent on taking the bus or subsistence. There was, as always, no contest. And the journey on foot continued.

After the "high" that had been engendered by his success, C.K. found himself gradually descending into a low place. It may have been the case that after many years of intense studying, culminating in the last major push and a Scholarship place at the highest school in the land, C.K. experienced a period of being detached from his school work. He may have been "burnt out", deflated, or depressed. But he was at the time an adolescent, a transitional, and for some testing cycle between childhood and adulthood when hormones are at play and the young endeavour to establish their independence. It could also be a confusing stage with regard to sexuality or sense of self. And in C.K.'s case, his disadvantaged family circumstances and unresolved issues regarding his paternity may have been magnified during this particular period.

The situation was undoubtedly exacerbated by the fact that even though C.K. had earned himself a place in the desired school, he was nonetheless in a learning environment where the majority had been products of better-off two-parent families who resided in the town of St George. Many whose families lived in country areas were boarded out within the town during term time. Others made the daily return trip by bus. But C.K. may have been one of the few students at the GBSS of the day whose journey involved a six-mile daily walk. It was undoubtedly a tiring trek for someone whose educational curriculum had been widened and was as a consequence significantly more demanding.

Despite the experienced difficulties, C.K. adjusted well at the Grenada Boys' Secondary School, where he made many new acquaintances but very few friends. And although he had been elevated onto a higher educational level, his true buddies remained Chasley David and Johnnie Bullen, who accompanied each other on the daily walk to school.

As the three pals arrived at their adolescence, they began to develop a keen interest in girls. Suddenly, the previous boisterous boys' only related banter had been replaced with the sharing of exaggerated outpourings about particular attractive girls, a favourite topic of conversation that was most probably peppered with considerable amounts of fantasising, fabrication, wishful thinking, but very little actuality. Even so, the displayed bravado could have been, in some cases, camouflage for secret love crushes.

C.K. had been at the time on friendly terms with a family who lived across the river and just beyond the village of Morne Delice. The family consisted of five siblings and was headed by their widowed mother, Juliana Banfield, commonly known as Cousin Doo Doo. Cousin Doo Doo was described as being short and plump and a friendly and jolly soul. She wore large broad-brimmed hats and was rarely seen without her apron with its extra-large pockets into which products picked from her garden were often secured. Whether or not C.K. had all along been smitten with one of Cousin Doo Doo's beautiful daughters was yet to be revealed.

In the meantime, C.K.'s long-held desire to assist struggling pupils with their school work had not diminished. And he would one day realise that his intelligence had been a valuable gift that could be exploited for earning a little extra pocket money. C.K. decided, while still at school, that he would deliver private tuition, one day a week, in the tiny "straw house" he shared with his mother for a fee of a single shilling per month. On being informed of her son's idea, Albertha did not hesitate in giving her consent to the initiative, nor did she object to the proposed tuition sessions taking place within the family's humble abode. Although the initial venture had been without doubt prompted by financial need, it could also have signalled an entrepreneur spirit with wings that would one day fly.

The proposed service was advertised by word of mouth and both C.K. and his mother were pleasantly surprised when the fee-paying private tuition classes attracted a number of "take ups" and proved successful. One of the various paying students was a classmate of C.K. by the name of Julius Isaac, who was tutored in mathematics.

C.K. could hardly believe how many "shillings" he had collected at the end of one month of tutoring. For the first time in his life he was handling "big money" which was his to spend however he chose and he was uplifted by a profound sense of self-worth. The money earned was in stark contrast to the meagre daily one penny allowance he received. And most significantly, there were twenty-four pennies in one shilling! Not surprisingly, C.K felt that he had been elevated into a different league altogether and was now a "rich man". Nonetheless, he would spend his earnings wisely and the priority was putting money aside to enable the purchase of a bicycle.

The boyhood dream of owning a bicycle was realised when C.K. had eventually accumulated the required funds and was able to buy his very first pair of wheels, at the grand cost of £1.00. The feelings of excitement and self-satisfaction associated with the independent purchase knew no bounds. But the much-valued possession was regularly left in safekeeping with a friend whose family home bordered "the river", or stretch of water which had been pathway to the village of Morne Delice. C.K. was not prepared to risk his cherished possession being damaged by riding through the tide. Moreover, carrying the bicycle across the river may have also been considered too hazardous an undertaking.

Although C.K. used his knowledge to assist others and at the same time earn additional cash, it was nevertheless during a period when his own studies were being neglected. But his personal difficulties were most probably made worse by the daily exhaustive six-mile school journey. C.K. says, "I spent five years at the Secondary School and I must confess that I did not end up too good a scholar." He added, "I must state at this stage I lived in St Paul's and the Secondary School was in St George's, three miles away, and I had to walk to and from school every day."

But what may have appeared a continuing lack of interest suddenly changed when the scheduled dates of the final examinations loomed near. The time for "stepping up to the plate" had arrived. Failure was not an option that C.K. was willing to consider. He was immediately jolted into gear and was once again a dedicated school student who focused totally on his work, with the end goal of attaining successful examination results.

Having fully completed even more than the required preparatory work, C.K. faced his final examination papers with confidence and was competent in every set module. He would not be disappointed. After a long and anxious wait for the results, he was elated. He had successfully obtained a pass in all Cambridge examination papers taken. C.K. says, "I left school in 1940 after passing the Senior Cambridge Examinations."

Albertha was triumphant. After many years of enduring hard work and sacrifice, she had reached the end of a very long road and had at last achieved her goal. She had done everything in her power to create the platform from which her son could be propelled onwards and upwards to a successful life. Albertha wept with joy and thanked God for C.K.'s academic attainments. But it was now her very own time to exhale. For the people who lived in the impoverished village of Morne Delice, C.K.'s achievements had been staggering. None amongst them had ever received such an accolade.

THE WORLD OF WORK

Albertha's job was finally over. She had done everything within her capabilities to ensure the educational foundation that was intended to open doors for her son. And even though the house in which he was raised had been precariously built, it was nonetheless the home in which he received good care, encouragement, security and stability. However it was not within Albertha's control to provide a substitute father or even a dependable male influence in C.K.'s life. Nor, it seemed, were his "stars" so aligned. But how C.K. may have wished he had a father who could have offered advice and guidance as he took his first lonely steps into an adult world.

And so it was that in the year 1940, C.K., aged 17, left school with Cambridge Examination Certificates under his belt but with no particular aspiration or career plan in mind. Nonetheless, his aim was to find himself paid employment but, disappointingly, every application submitted was unsuccessful. All the while C.K. was continuing to deliver private tuition at the meagre fee of one shilling a month.

FROM HUMBLE BEGINNINGS

After twelve months of repeated job-seeking failures, one of C.K.'s childhood friends, Chasley David, suggested that he should join him at the Grenada Telephone Company, which at the time was run by the Government. In those early days of communication technology on the island of Grenada, all telephones came with an attached handle and were linked to a central switchboard. Making a call required a three-stage process. Firstly, a privately-owned telephone would be activated by vigorous turns of the attached handle. This action triggered a ringing tone which alerted the Central Operator to pick up at his or her end. And the caller was at this third stage connected by the Operator to the number requested.

Although Chasley had been employed as a telephone apprentice, he did not receive a salary, but was nonetheless grateful for the training and work experience delivered. After many months of working for "no pay", Chasley was advised by his employers that the situation was about to change and that he would be placed on a salary of one shilling a day. It was the point at which Chasley advised his friend C.K. to apply for an apprenticeship position with the Grenada Telephone Company as he also should receive the proposed salary.

It was to C.K.'s huge relief that his application was successful and before too long he was being trained in repairing telephones and telephone lines alongside his friend Chasley, on a similar salary of one shilling a day. He had at long last "broken the ice" and would go on to being successful in all future employment applications. But C.K. had no particular career aspiration and would be carried along a working road of twists and turns that would eventually lead to a totally unexpected destination.

Even though C.K. had no specific teaching training, he had for many years assisted less able children with their school work and also delivered fee-paying private tuition to various individuals who sought to further their education. He was, as a consequence, an experienced albeit unofficial teacher, and it was the basis on which he applied for a teaching position at one of the Government Primary schools. C.K.'s application was successful and he was offered a teaching post at a salary of £2.00 a month. Thrilled by the prospect of an increased wage for doing something he loved, C.K. resigned from the Telephone Company after just one year into his apprenticeship. The year was 1942.

Teaching was C.K.'s vocation from which he received the personal satisfaction of doing something he felt was worthwhile. And being able to enable the learning process and guide and monitor the educational progression of his young pupils had been a most rewarding experience. But after nearly two years in the teaching profession, C.K. was seduced into returning to the Telephone Company when he was offered a job as a Telephone Assistant at what at the time was considered a very good monthly wage of £3.65. This was almost double the amount he was being paid in his position as Primary School Teacher.

C.K. had returned to the Grenada Telephone Company for only a few short months when he was given the opportunity of a highly-paid job with an oil company on the island of Curacao. It was in the year 1946 and C.K., who was at the time just 23 years old felt that he could not "turn down" the chance of what appeared to be an open door into a lucrative economic future. This coincided with a period when large numbers of young men and women were leaving the island of Grenada and seeking their fortune in foreign countries. Consequently, close friends and family members, including his mother Albertha, supported C.K.'s decision to accept the offer of a work position overseas.

Despite the general optimism and good wishes, C.K. was unable to control being gripped by a sad sinking feeling in his stomach as he waved goodbye to close family members and friends before leaving the island of his birth for the very first time. Nonetheless, like many young people of his day, C.K. was with considerable anticipation seeking a better life abroad and had no intention of returning to Grenada any time soon.

FREE AT LAST

Albertha was of the opinion that C.K.'s take-up of a job on the island of Curacao, would be a permanent move. Why would he want to return to Grenada? Albertha felt sure C.K. would move on to much better things on the island of opportunity. She reasoned that nearly everyone with ambition was heading for other Caribbean islands such as Trinidad and Tobago, Aruba and Curacao in search of economic openings. And that her son was luckier than most because he would be going straight into a job. What could be better? It was a good feeling. It was now "me" time. Albertha would no longer have to prepare meals for her son or do his laundry. He had left home and she was free to live her life as she pleased.

Albertha decided that she would start her life afresh on the island of Trinidad. But there was a problem. She did not possess the full fare required for the boat journey, so she came up with the plan to simply stow away. Always a single-minded and focused character, Albertha sneaked fearlessly and unnoticed onto a vessel headed for the island of choice and was somehow able to remain invisible until she alighted, unscathed, on the pier of the land of opportunity. It had been undoubtedly a brave and courageous undertaking. Albertha experienced very little difficulty adjusting to her new life on the larger and relatively prosperous island of Trinidad. She relished in being a free and independent woman whose priority had shifted from the needs of her only son to those of her own. Albertha was resolute in taking care of "No 1" and by "the grace of God" looked forward to an anticipated bright new future. It was not too long before Albertha's rosy prediction became a reality when she was taken on as housekeeper at the home of who was then the most popular and highly-regarded tailor on the island of Trinidad; and at a salary that was way above what she had ever previously earned. Albertha could not have been happier and thanked God for her good fortune.

THE TURNING POINT

C.K. arrived on the island of Curaçao in a positive frame of mind. Here he was, a young man on the cusp of an independent life on an island that promised economic opportunity. Indeed, a job with a lucrative salary was already on hold for him and he expected a matched overall lifestyle. There was no denying C.K.'s optimism as he embarked on what was envisaged to be the right path for ensuring a successful future.

As time went on, the novelty of living on a relatively progressive island and being able to earn "good money" began to wear thin. C.K. increasingly came to the realisation that something was missing as he struggled to adjust to a new country and, for him, an alien culture. C.K. yearned for his familiar home surroundings and most of all missed his close friends. And even though he was being paid a large wage, the money was not enough. It seemed that not even time – the great healer – could heal his deepening home-sickness, which also appeared to have affected his physical health. For the first time in his life, C.K. felt continually unwell.

FROM HUMBLE BEGINNINGS

After two years working on the island of Curacao, C.K. had had enough. He decided to follow his heart by returning to his home country, despite the limited scope for career opportunities. And stepping back on the land of his birth, in the year 1948, had been, for C.K. Sylvester, liberating. It was so good to be on home soil. He knew straight away that this was the place he wanted to be and was unable to wipe the smile off his face. He was once again a happy man. And all previous persistent symptoms of physical or emotional difficulties miraculously vanished.

C.K. would waste no time reconnecting with close family members and friends and everyone was delighted to welcome him home. Of the various persons C.K. visited on his return was Cousin Doo Doo. How could he ever forget the warm and friendly widowed mother of five who lived across the river? C.K. had developed a connection with Cousin Doo Doo and her family when he was just a boy. He was in the same age group as Doo Doo's children and loved their homely family environment into which he was at all times welcomed. As the years passed by, C.K. found that he was being drawn to one of Doo Doo's pretty daughters. She was called Vernice and was the middle child of the siblings. C.K. and Vernice developed a firm friendship and their interactions were easy-flowing and spontaneous.

The saying "Absence makes the heart grow fonder" would have been fitting for a man who found himself thinking constantly of the girl he left behind all the while he was in Curacao. She was for him a young lady like no other and coming face to face with the heart's desire after two long years apart had been a pivotal moment. Vernice Banfield was struck by the dashing young man standing before her. Dressed in casual but smart designer menswear of the day, C.K. at that moment could easily have been mistaken for "a passing tourist". Didn't realise he was so breathtakingly handsome, Vernice thought. But C.K. had been equally impressed. The pretty young girl he so often visualised during long lonely nights spent on the island of Curacao had blossomed into a beautiful young woman. It was an undoubted magical few seconds as the long-time friends clasped hands and charmed each other with beaming smiles that were enhanced by two pairs of eyes that sparkled reciprocally.

And when at a subsequent stolen private moment C.K. declared his undying love, Vernice was overcome with happiness, but affirmed in a shy manner that she loved him too. The embrace that followed was highly charged with the impassioned intensity of two young people who were for the first time experiencing true love. It would be the first of many blissfully passionate moments shared by the couple.

It was not long before C.K. expressed honourable intentions to his heart's desire and, in line with expectations of the day, respectfully asked the widowed Cousin Doo Doo for her daughter's hand in marriage. And to the couple's joyful relief, the matriarch willingly and without hesitation nodded while verbally reinforcing her approval. Cousin Doo Doo had always been fond of C.K. and was very pleased that he now aspired to be her son-in-law. He was a man with "prospects" and she could not have wished for a better husband for her beloved daughter.

The breaking news of the romance could have been received with an element of déjà vu among those who harboured the long-held suspicion that C.K. had for some time been secretly enamoured by one of Cousin Doo Doo's attractive daughters. These "meddlesome" individuals, and there were many in those days, could imagine no other compelling reason for C.K.'s previous frequent visits to Doo Doo's family home; and consequently were not surprised by the revelation that happily confirmed their thinking.

Soon the excitement of the wedding planning would tighten its grip as the family rallied to organise C.K. and Vernice's special day. The marriage ceremony took place at the local Roman Catholic

Church. It was a small gathering consisting mainly of close family members and friends, with Maria Clyne, daughter of C.K.'s half-sister Dreda, being the chief bridesmaid. The newly-married couple and their guests posed cheerfully as photographs were taken, before returning to the reception venue. At the end of the speeches, everyone tucked into the eagerly-awaited food and drink. But the highlight of the evening was the cutting of the beautifully-decorated wedding cake by the newly-married couple, while wild applause escalated to its crescendo; and glasses were raised as everyone joined in wishing the couple a long and happy marriage. It had been the most memorable of days.

C.K. and Vernice would begin their life together at the home of the bride's mother, Cousin Doo Doo.

The year of 1948 marked a significant turning point in C.K.'s life. It was the year he abandoned the idea of a new life in Curacao and returned home, even though it was during a period when opportunities were limited and many were migrating abroad. But he was happy to have reclaimed his sense of belonging in the place and among those with whom he felt most comfortable. To crown it all, he had married the love of his life and moreover was offered a position as a Store Clerk at a retail company known as Gerald S.W. Smith & Co. Ltd. By then the national currency had changed from Sterling to Caribbean dollars and C.K. was being paid a monthly salary of $20.00. Everything appeared to be falling into place and there were no regrets regarding the decision to "go back". But had C.K. been led simply by his heart or was the backward turn onto a road previously judged to be a "dead end" engineered by the hand of fate? The answer was yet to unfold.

STEPPING STONES

It was like a "duck in water" that C.K. cruised effortlessly and without pressure on home territory. He had given up the chance of an economically-profitable future in exchange for a happy life. And he did indeed find the happiness he craved. C.K. was satisfied in his position as a Store Clerk and in particular looked forward to returning to a loving wife and associated home comforts at the end of the working day. What more could a man ask for? But unbeknown to C.K., his Manager at the retail company had spotted his potential. It was a time when he had no particular work ambition and endeavoured only to apply himself to the work at hand. Consequently, even though he had no previous experience of working in the commercial field, C.K. adapted quickly and his work performance was assessed to be reliably efficient and effective. But any idea that he may have been en route to finding his true calling had not even entered his psyche.

After one year of employment as a Store Clerk, C.K. was pleasantly surprised when he was rewarded for consistently producing excellent work by being promoted to the position of Travelling Salesman at the doubled salary of $40.00 monthly. The job involved travelling by boat throughout the Windward and Leeward Caribbean islands, where he was tasked with procuring business transactions for his company. And, equipped with a sound knowledge base of his product, communication skills developed over many years spent in the teaching profession and general inter-personal attributes, C.K. would seek out prospective foreign customers and competently negotiate and secure profitable deals on behalf of his company. Moreover, the gratification derived from the process had been nothing less than exhilarating. It was the first inkling that C.K. may have, without knowing, landed on the home stretch to his destiny.

But, as always, there was a negative side. And it came in the form of having to be absent from home for several months at a time. It was nonetheless a price C.K. and his wife Vernice were willing to pay. The couple, who had been living at the home of Cousin Doo Doo, aspired to have a place of their own, and consequently welcomed the salary increase for enabling the funds necessary for hastening the day when they could thank the kindly Cousin Doo Doo for her hospitality before moving on with their lives.

C.K. had been employed as a travelling salesman for approximately four years when he was approached by a firm called James Milne Company and offered an identical position, with the lure of a $35.00 a month salary increase which resulted in a monthly income of $75.00. To be given the opportunity of continuing a job he loved and in which he excelled for significantly more money was an offer that no right-minded individual, such as C.K., could refuse.

Leo Cromwell had been one of several travelling salesmen employed by the James Milne Company. He explained that his colleagues were smartly outfitted, self-assured young men, but considerable emphasis was placed on having a good time.

They travelled on Federal boats. These were "luxury steamships" that had been donated by the Canadian Government and they carried not only sales personnel but also passengers to and from the islands of Trinidad and Jamaica. Among the passengers were beautiful and flirtatious young women who did not object to brief dalliances with the dashing young salesmen. And as the working schedule required six months on ship and six months off, wives and partners at home were temporarily forgotten as the men became captivated by the various attractive young passengers of the opposite sex. C.K. was, however, the sole exception. He was never a womaniser and appeared oblivious to the female beauties that attempted to attract his attention. Leo described C.K. as being at the time a faithful and devoted husband who loved his family. Apart from being fundamentally kind and considerate with never a bad word to say about anyone, Leo went on to say that his friend and co-worker was also an honest, straightforward and hardworking individual whose main focus was the job in hand.

During periods spent on land, the sharply-dressed, self-assured clique of young salesmen stood out from the crowd as they swaggered through the streets of the town of St George. The "hip" young men would regularly join each other in their favourite record shop on Saturday afternoon, where they would get into the groove and tap their feet to the rhythms and beat while popular sounds of the day such as jazz and smooth were being "blasted" at high volume.

The men also shared good times accompanied by their respective wives or partners. Leo said that the group consisted of six couples and they participated together in social activities such as parties, picnics on the beach or weekend breaks at a hotel of choice. C.K., on those occasions, was reported to be very much a fun person. He enjoyed music, dancing, cracking jokes and general socialising. And his laughter resounded as heartily as the rest.

THE YOUNG FAMILY

After their marriage in 1948, the newly-wedded couple began their life together at the house of the bride's mother, Cousin Doo Doo. C.K. had not too long returned to the island from Curaçao and even though he succeeded in finding employment, the couple were unable to afford the costs involved with renting a place of their own during the initial stages of their union. But C.K. and Vernice were happy. They were very much in love and Cousin Doo Doo allowed them the space and privacy to enjoy abandoned passionate moments. It was indeed a sublime period and the couple's happiness was sealed by the arrival of their first-born just one year after their marriage.

Everyone was thrilled with the new addition to the family and agreed that the tiny girl was a real little beauty. Indeed, when the first-time parents were visited by the local Catholic Priest, he appeared captivated by the infant and remarked on how "cute" she was. The well-received comment had been reinforcement to the family that they were not being simply partial in judging one of their own beautiful. It was an opinion also shared by a well-respected Priest. And from that time onwards the new baby was in dulcet tones referred to as "Cutie". And even though she would be subsequently officially named Yolande, the pet name stuck and she would from the moment of the Father's endearing compliment, always be known as "Cutie".

Subsequent to his second promotion to the post of Travelling Salesman with a further hike in wages, C.K. could at last afford to move his young family into rented accommodation at the cost of $20.00 a month. Vernice welcomed being mistress in her own home for the first time since her marriage two years previously. It seemed a long time coming, but she was now free to independently organise her household. But long separations from her husband because of his job as a Travelling Salesman resulted in many lonely nights. Vernice missed C.K. dreadfully and would tick off the days until his return. But during periods when the young husband was back on home ground, the couple made up for lost time and were inseparable. Within two years of giving birth to their first child, C.K. and Vernice produced a second beautiful baby girl, whom they called Cecily. C.K. was enchanted by his little angel at the very first sight. He found the infant compelling and she was "daddy's little girl" from that day onwards.

The longed-for son and heir for ensuring the continuation of the family name was also conceived at the rented house. The newly-born infant was named Phillip Kenrick, after his father. He appeared at a time when C.K. had resigned from his post as Travelling Salesman for one company but was employed in the same capacity by another, with a significant increase in salary. And by the year 1954, the family had accumulated enough savings for a down payment on building a home of their own. The purpose-built house erected on purchased land was large and spacious. It consisted of three bedrooms, living room, dining and kitchen areas and laundry facilities. The house also boasted a study and servants' quarters. The remaining cost of the project was paid in full on completion.

On the day prior to the date that had been set for moving into the new property, Grenada was struck by a catastrophic hurricane which resulted in landslides, flooding, flattened buildings and a significant number of lost lives. The family had not, however, been seriously affected by the storm and the newly-built house sustained only minor damage to its exterior. As a consequence, they were able to move out of rented accommodation and into their very own family home just one day after the originally-planned date in September 1955. The new building had been a far cry from the humble two-room hut that had been constructed with cardboard and straw and in which C.K. had been raised. At the time of becoming a first-time private home owner, C.K. was 32 years of age.

The family remained close and when C.K. was not working abroad, the devoted husband and father would take his family on rides in their Ford Anglia. It had been C.K.'s first car and purchased when the family lived in their rented house. They would drive around the island on a Sunday afternoon and linger in places of interest. They also visited relatives or friends who resided in country areas, but the siblings particularly enjoyed spending time with their grandmother, Cousin Doo Doo. They looked forward to being fed hot "leaven bread" with the distinctive taste that comes with being freshly baked on "fig leaves" inside an outdoor brick oven; and, served with the customary seasoned home-made black pudding, it was the most deliciously flavoursome meal.

C.K. and Vernice continued to operate a conventional family lifestyle as the years went by and the children grew older. Vernice was described as being friendly and jovial, with a great sense of humour. But she also carried a wise and philosophical head on her slender shoulders and would at the drop of a hat reinforce any particular life situation by quoting an appropriate proverb. And her belief in Fate was qualified by the words: "what is to is, must is." But Vernice was first and foremost a dutiful wife who presented very little challenges to her husband, whom she loved dearly. Their offspring were equally precious. And although being essentially a loving and nurturing mother who took very good care of the children, she maintained consistent firmness in relation to expectations, values and boundaries. Overall, Mrs Vernice Sylvester was a committed wife and mother who ensured that the family home was at all times smoothly run.

For his part, C.K. was a responsible husband and father who loved his home and family. But he could be, on occasions, inflexible in his dealings with the children, which more than likely indicated that the relatively privileged lifestyle they enjoyed should not be taken for granted; a thinking that was most probably rooted in memories of childhood experiences of being raised within a deprived and poverty-stricken community. Despite these factors, requests from younger daughter, Cecily, for whom C.K. carried a "soft spot", were rarely if ever refused. He seemed somehow unable to say "no" to his little princess. But far from being envious, the remaining siblings viewed the sister's special relationship with their father as being advantageous, and ensured their favours were granted by persuading "daddy's girl" to intervene on their behalf.

But C.K. was a conscientious, hard-working, responsible and reliable provider who made sure that his family's needs were being fully met. In the event, the family wanted for nothing. C.K. and Vernice together created a home environment that was warm and welcoming, and where the children were happy and safely protected, with their strong Catholic Faith being integral to the family's lifestyle. And so it was, daily routines in the Sylvester household ticked along nicely and seemed forever. The fact that life is an unpredictable journey may have been, in those glory years, an unimaginable reality.

In parallel to sustaining a happy and functional family life, C.K.'s career continued to move in an upwards and onwards direction.

DESTINY ROAD

After many years of being a competent and highly-productive Travelling Salesman, it was not unnoticed by his employer that he had been a valuable asset to the company, and he was rewarded for his exceptional performance by being promoted to the position of Assistant Managing Director. It was the point at which the company's name was changed from James Milne Company to James Milne (Grenada) Ltd.; the Managing Director being Mr James Kenrick Milne.

Once again C.K. found himself at the deep end of unchartered waters. He had received no training, preparation or even experience for the senior position to which he was being appointed. But he had been given the opportunity to demonstrate, on the highest level, his capabilities, skills and attributes and he would grab the chance firmly and with both hands. So, equipped with a sound academic background, God-given intelligence and work experiences, particularly in ensuring business contracts for the company, C.K. braced himself in readiness for tackling the challenges that lay ahead. The year was 1960 and he was 37 years of age.

Adjusting into the role of Assistant Managing Director presented no difficulties for C.K. Sylvester. Administration procedures proved unproblematic and it was not very long before his feet were firmly planted under the desk. C.K.'s work ethics were second to none. He was energised by the challenges that came with his new position of responsibility and he applied the time and effort that was necessary for contributing fully to the steady growth of the company.

The successes enjoyed by the company following C.K.'s managerial appointment resulted in his employer being confident in the Assistant Director's capabilities with regard to the operation of the business. And when Mr Milne decided to leave Grenada and reside overseas, C.K. agreed to the proposal that he would replace Mr Milne and assume the position of Managing Director, along with 25% of the company's shares.

The autonomy that was synonymous with the role of Managing Director resulted in boosted motivation in endeavours for achieving profitable outcomes for the company. And over subsequent years and in the absence of input of any kind from the owner, Mr Milne, the company expanded and profits increased by huge margins. But C.K. became increasingly disgruntled, as even though he had put in the work that resulted in the company's profits that contributed greatly to the owner's comfortable lifestyle, C.K. was of the opinion that he was not being fairly remunerated, as the 25% of the shares he was originally granted remained unchanged.

On expressing an intention to resign from the company as he did not feel that he was being fully appreciated or rewarded, C.K.'s second wife, who had for many years worked as his secretary and in so doing had acquired an in-depth knowledge of the business, made the suggestion that he should set up his own company. The idea not only registered but it felt as though a switch had been turned on and was radiating through his brain. After more than twenty years of proceeding down a very long road, C.K. had suddenly collided with his true calling and that experiences encountered along the way may have been preparatory lessons for this specific moment. There could be no denying that he had been steered along the right path, but nothing happens before the decreed time.

It was a point in time when C.K. felt rejuvenated by the idea of being master of his own enterprise. He would embrace the prospect with a renewed sense of purpose, drive and enthusiasm. After many years of being an employee, he was about to become an independent agent. And in reflecting that fact, C.K. would name his bold business adventure "Independence Agencies". The year was 1973 and he was 50 years old. Thirty-five years or more had elapsed since he had unknowingly glimpsed his destiny. C.K. was only a schoolboy when he was struck with the idea that much-needed funds could be acquired from providing private tuition in the "straw house" he shared with his mother. The initiative was implemented and proved successful.

LOVE AND LOSS

The year that delivered a new and exciting business initiative also brought in its wake devastating personal loss.

The marital relationship between C.K. and Vernice had been based on love, friendship and respect for each other. The couple shared the desire of sustaining a stable and secure upbringing for their children. In so doing, C.K. held responsibility for being the provider while Vernice remained the homemaker. Both parties were committed in their separate roles and together succeeded in providing the desired family environment.

The family were joined for a time by C.K.'s mother Albertha when she returned to Grenada after many years of working on the island of Trinidad. Mother and son had maintained contact with each other via letter-writing and Albertha had been amazed to hear of C.K.'s extraordinary successes. He had achieved so much more than she ever imagined and she was immensely proud. C.K. re-paid his mother for the sacrifices she made in ensuring he received the best education available by presenting her with a newly-built house. But although Albertha was thrilled to be the first-time owner of a property of worth, her son's exceptional successes had been without doubt the prevailing greatest reward.

Despite the normal disagreements that may occur between couples, C.K. and Vernice remained happy together over many years in a relationship that may have been driven by the seemingly unwavering chemistry between them. But as the years went by C.K. became more absorbed in his work and less interested in the personal relationship with his wife. He would leave for the office at the crack of dawn and after a long day would be grumpy on his return home. Considerable periods would also be spent in "The Club", where allegedly large quantities of alcohol were consumed. And C.K. would apparently arrive home, worse for drink, and create "merry hell" with his wife who at no time retaliated but simply removed herself from his presence by entering and locking herself in a separate room. Although his anger was never physically manifested, Vernice nonetheless endured the emotional and psychological consequences of C.K.'s unreasonable behaviour.

Although the love and respect once held for his wife appeared to have been eroded, Vernice's love for her husband was undiminished and she continued to be the dutiful wife. But she was able to find solace by pursuing personal interests and hobbies such as gardening and fishing. She was a keen and expert gardener who was able to produce roses of five different colours on a single tree. A sense of peace and serenity was also derived from fishing, a hobby shared with son Ken, and the pair would spend hours together participating in their favourite activity. Unable to fathom the joy of fishing, C.K. decided to accompany his wife and son on one of their fishing expeditions, but his involvement lasted only minutes. C.K. excluded himself after very quickly deciding that, for him, fishing was nothing but dull and boring.

Apart from being occupied with hobbies and interests, Vernice made various charitable contributions to the local community. She organised Christmas parties for the local children and ran an ice cream stall at the annual Church Harvest, with all takings being donated to charitable causes.

In the year 1961, an Italian cruiser called the *Bianca C* with 600 passengers and crewmen caught fire after an explosion and subsequently sank in close proximity to St George's harbour. There were just two fatalities and survivors were rescued by the Emergency Services and locals and were taken to hotels, guest houses or private homes. Vernice was among those who rushed to the scene and organised transportation to places of safety.

All the while Vernice continued in her efforts to avoid the breakdown of her marriage. She would remind herself of the marriage vows and, in particular, the line which states: "for better or worse"; and despite the experienced turbulence, Vernice considered it part of the course and that the situation would eventually be overcome. In the meantime, she remained stoic and made no demands of her spouse, and would "take the bus" even to and from hospital appointments. On the other hand, Vernice lovingly prepared her husband's favourite dish such as "pig foot souse" or "sea eggs". Sea eggs would be carefully selected on fishing trips and made tastefully palatable by being seasoned with local herbs and peppers. C.K. often took his favourite meal to work to be eaten at lunch. And Vernice was always reassured that the favourite meal had been eaten and enjoyed by the emptied dish that was returned at the end of the day.

But Vernice's mind was opened to the possibility that someone else may also have been participating in the carefully-prepared favourite dish. It was the day daughter "Cutie" revealed that she had spotted her father at his secretary's front door and that she handed him the exact dish which contained the "sea eggs" that had been specifically prepared for his lunch that day. The unexpected revelation left Vernice reeling with shock. Suddenly everything began to fall into place. The lack of interest, argumentative outpourings and general unreasonable behaviours had been, in retrospect, indicators that her husband had been having an affair with his secretary. Vernice may have scolded herself for being so blind and naively trusting, but she was no less deeply hurt by the act of betrayal. Vernice did not confront her husband with the allegation that had been made by their daughter. She decided at that point to remain calm and wait for things to take their natural course, which she believed could never be changed. "What is to is, must is." Her only outward reaction would be to cease the practice of preparing her husband's favourite dishes.

The once happy and fulfilling relationship between C.K. and Vernice continued its downward slide and at a time when C.K.'s career was flying high and going from strength to strength, and during a period when the family's finances were better than ever and a second larger home had been built. Nonetheless, their affluent material lifestyle contrasted starkly with the emotional tension that weighed heavily within the home environment. And the day eventually arrived when the couple acknowledged that their union was beyond redemption and decided that they should go their separate ways after 18 long years of married life.

But subsequent to their separation, C.K. realised his mistakes and made repeated unsuccessful attempts at reconciliation. He was at heart a family man who loved his wife and children and had no desire to live separately from them. He regretted being carried away by the intoxicating demands related to his work commitments and being swayed by the charms of the person with whom he worked closely and that he had taken his wife for granted. Nonetheless, Vernice, a philosophical soul who believed in Fate, commented: "Men: you can't live with them and you can't live without them"; but "what is to is, must is", and there was as a consequence no going back. As far as Vernice was concerned, trust had vanished from what was considered a fundamentally solid marital relationship despite the experienced difficulties.

C.K. says, "Vernice divorced me because of the relationship I had." The couple were indeed divorced in the year 1968. And the happy family life once filled with promises of forever was sadly no more.

C.K. would go on to marry his secretary and continued to exert considerable time and energy in his job.

The saying "true love never dies" had been without doubt applicable with regard to C.K. and Vernice, even though they were divorced and had moved on with their separate lives. In her own right, Vernice had been a fundamentally strong and independently-minded woman and she went on to own and manage a profit-making Boutique. She also continued to pursue her hobbies of fishing and gardening and was generally socially active.

On becoming unwell, Vernice acted on medical advice and entered hospital for a routine gynaecological procedure. But following the operation that was determined successful, Vernice appeared despondent and resisted all attempts that were being made to aid a speedy recovery. She refused, categorically, offers of assistance in getting out of her hospital bed and declined engaging in simple exercise. It was generally felt that although Vernice had been putting on a brave face, she had never totally recovered from her failed marriage, and in her vulnerable state had been gripped by an episode of depression resulting in an apparent lack of will or desire to carry on. But just one day after delighting her family by appearing cheery and uplifted, Vernice unexpectedly fell unconscious in her hospital bed and could not be revived. Vernice was just 47 years of age when she was taken by a blood clot which had lodged in her lungs. The entire family were shocked and shattered. C.K. in particular was a broken man. He had lost the love of his life. The year was 1973.

OFFSPRING PERCEPTIONS

As a man who never knew his father nor was recompensed by having a substitute father in his life, C.K., as a consequence, had no role model on which his own fathering techniques could be based. He was nonetheless conscientious in parenting his own children and endeavoured to be always "there" for them. In so doing he worked hard and succeeded in being a consistently responsible and reliable father who was deeply committed to ensuring the safety and well-being of his offspring. And the siblings were able to enjoy a relatively privileged upbringing within a stable, secure and comfortable home environment.

Although C.K. was also raised up in a secure and stable home, it was in abject poverty and within a humble unsupported single-parent household that lacked all material comforts. Consequently, the hand-to-mouth existence experienced, in conjunction with the enduring emotional emptiness associated with the absent parent, would no doubt have left an indelible mark on the young boy. And to some extent may have "coloured" his personal parenting approaches.

As a young boy, C.K. was perceived as being a stern parent by eldest son Ken. He recalled that his father once bought him a motor-cycle, but suggested that he should earn the cash for repaying the cost of the motor-cycle by renting it out. Ken received no sympathy on expressing his intention to use his brand new bike for riding to school and alleged being told, in no uncertain terms, that he must continue "walking" to school. Daughter Cutie also had a story to tell. She said that on request to borrow "the car", the response would always be a lecture on the wear and tear of tyres, price of gasoline and general ongoing costs of vehicle maintenance. But on one particular occasion a visiting friend who overheard her father's tirade intervened with the words, "Man, don't be so stupid", closely followed by, "Girl, just take the car and go." Needless to say, Cutie immediately grabbed the car keys and hurriedly exited the house.

These particular examples of parenting methods may have had a bearing on childhood experiences that lingered beneath the surface. Due to lack of funds, C.K. had no choice but to undertake a six-mile school journey on foot five days a week over many years. It was the reason also that he independently earned the money required for purchasing his first bicycle. C.K. had been raised within a materially poverty-stricken community and shared the struggles of the people. But even though he ensured that his own children benefited from receiving everything they needed, he also delivered lessons in avoiding dependency by endeavouring to be independent, and never always expecting to have things handed on a plate. These were undeniably fundamental life principles that C.K. was determined to instil into the mindset of his offspring. How well he knew that the lifestyle the family enjoyed had been hard-earned over many years of continued diligent working; an assertion underlined by Ken when he revealed childhood observations. Ken alleged that his father was "always busy" and acted like a "workaholic".

Nevertheless, C.K. appeared helpless when it came to his younger daughter, Cecily. He was putty in her hands and she was granted every request without hesitation. But that fact had in no way impacted negatively on the siblings' close relationships with each other. Moreover, daddy's little girl could always be relied upon to apply her winsome charms in ways that would benefit her brother and sister.

Cutie revealed fond memories of when she would accompany her father to the New Year's Eve ball festivities. Father and daughter always danced with each other to the first tune played after the dawning of the New Year had been gleefully celebrated with song, mutual embraces and general "fanfare". Cutie was also partnered by C.K. on the night of her Graduation Ball. She felt proud to be walking into the venue on the arm of her father, with whom she also danced on that memorable night.

Despite the indicators which suggested that C.K may have had a favourite child, the siblings were secure in the knowledge that they were loved equally by their father. Both Cutie and Ken recalled as children being taken on family day trips by their father and that he was never known to have shied away from "pushing the pram" at a time when it was not generally considered the manly thing to do. Indeed, their father ensured that everything was evenly distributed among the siblings; a fact underlined by Ken when he said that C.K. had been "a fair father".

It was clearly apparent that the siblings deeply loved, appreciated and were proud of their responsible and fair-minded father, who had been consistent in ensuring and protecting their best interests. They were also proud of their father as an individual in his own right, and proud of what he achieved.

FLYING HIGH WITH INDEPENDENCE AGENCIES

The devastatingly heart-rending loss of his first wife, followed by the birth of a new career, had been contrasting life-changing events that occurred in the life of C.K. Sylvester during the fateful year of 1973. But despite being burdened by a broken heart, C.K. could not ignore the fact that, at the relatively late stage in his life, he had discovered what was felt to be his true calling, and wasted little time in submitting his resignation and embracing the challenges involved with the launching of a business. He had for a considerable period exerted great efforts into managing and expanding a company on behalf of the absent employer, and it was with many years of relevant experience under his belt and a passionate desire to succeed that C.K. held the reins of his very own enterprise. The fact that many long-standing satisfied customers pledged their allegiance by deciding to transfer to the new company had undoubtedly been a "start-up" advantage.

After many years of being an employee, all constraints, restrictions and frustrations had been lifted. C.K. had become his own "boss". He was at long last an independent operator, and in reflection of his newly-acquired status, named his company Independence Agencies Limited.

C.K. says, "My original plan was that Independence Agencies Limited would have been a family business." This was confirmed by son Ken, who said that he was one of the original three staff members which, apart from himself, included his father C.K. and a relative who was tasked with "driving the van" which delivered products to outlets up and down the island. It was during a period when the vehicle containing "the goods" could be parked unlocked anywhere and "no one would touch it".

After many years of assisting his father with running the Company, Ken migrated to Canada in 1979. During his time in Canada, Ken entered University and obtained a degree in Business Management. On his return to the homeland in 1988, Ken resumed his role as Assistant Director of Independence Agencies Limited. Shortly thereafter the Company purchased a local cinema which had been advertised for sale and it was converted into a sizeable warehouse and office.

Ken recalls accompanying his father when in 1994 a large building was being auctioned. C.K. had been advised of the proposed sale at auction after being for some time unsuccessfully seeking suitably spacious premises for accommodating his ever-expanding business. On the scheduled day and time of the auction, C.K. was one of just two prospective purchasers present, and as soon as the bidding process was initiated by the auctioneer, C.K. grabbed the moment and quickly stepped in with a substantial first bid. Attention was at that point directed to the only other interested person in expectation of an increased offer, but the response was astoundingly unexpected. The second prospective purchaser wasted no time in making it clear that he had been unable to surpass the first offer by declaring "pass". The surprisingly unexpected response resulted in a hasty end to the proceedings as the auctioneer promptly and forcefully struck the table with his gavel and delivered the determination, "Sold, to Mr Sylvester."

The building was at a later stage transformed into C.K.'s Super Valu Wholesale and Retail Outlet.

C.K.'s oldest daughter, Yolande, commonly known as Cutie, held the managerial position at C.K's Super Valu Food Depot, a cash-and-carry outlet. It was an extension of the company Independence Agencies Ltd. and was officially opened in February 1995.

Despite what may appear to have been Independence Agencies Limited's smooth upward flight to success, turbulence in the form of disappointment and financial loss had been experienced. In particular, C.K. would say that his greatest financial loss was the quarter of a million dollars paid in advance for the importing of a large shipment of sugar from a South American country. Not only did the paid-for shipment fail to arrive, but no reimbursement was made.

There were also personal losses during the period. The kindly and much-loved Cousin Doo Doo passed away on 18th March 1976 and C.K. lost his beloved mother from complications resulting from diabetes on 28th June 1987. Big "sister" Dreda Clyne also departed this life in the late 1980s. Marie, the younger of C.K.'s two sisters, would follow in the year 2000 at the age of 95.

The stresses of building a business were often relieved by visits, particularly on weekends, to "The Club", where C.K. would socialise and drink with other men of professional standing. Cutie admitted fearing for her father's life on a specific Saturday night/Sunday morning in 1981. C.K. had been returning home from "The Club" when he was involved in a serious accident while driving drunk. The scare resulted in Cutie engaging in a "heart to heart" talk with her father about his excessive consumption of alcohol and consequential risks. There was no doubting that the accident, compounded by Cutie's warnings, had been the wake-up call that signalled the end of C.K.'s drinking habit. Another drop of alcohol would never in the future pass his lips.

The historic and celebratory year of 1974 arrived at a time when Independence Agencies Limited was on the rise. On 7th February 1974, Grenada, along with the sister isles of Carriacou and Petite Martinique, was granted independence by the British Government, and the population as a whole was victorious. On a personal level, C.K. had been happy to put work aside in order to give his eldest daughter Cutie away when she married the scientist Dr Peter Martin Radix, also a well-known musician and music producer from the parish of St David, on 3rd June 1974. C.K. would subsequently fly to London, England, where he again performed his duty as a father by proudly walking younger daughter Cecily down the aisle at her marriage to Mr Brendon Batson, one of England's pioneering black Premier League footballers from St Patrick's, Grenada, on 15th June 1974. C.K. was delighted that both girls had married fine, upstanding young men.

The drive, enthusiasm and hard work being injected into Independence Agencies Ltd. by its founder C.K. Sylvester, for sustaining the efficiency and effectiveness of the company, continued unwaveringly for over thirty years.

Subsequent to retiring at the age of 80 in 2003, C.K. stated the following:

"I, Cecil K. Sylvester, established Independence Agencies Limited as Manufacturers Representatives, Commission Agents and Wholesalers in October 1973, and the company was registered on 20th October 1973. I borrowed $12,000.00 from the Royal Bank of Canada to finance the company and used my personal Insurance Policies as Security.

The office was located upstairs a building which was used as a dwelling house in Tyrell Street. The office space was two rooms and my staff number was three, including myself, but during the latter part of 1974 we moved to the Jaycees Building in Scott Street. The ground floor was used for Stock and Sales while the first floor was used as our office. The staff number was increased to five members.

The main source of income during the early stages was the use of a Sales-van operating in the country districts. The van was purchased with an additional loan of $8,000.00. In the meantime, the company succeeded in obtaining some agencies, so we started to book orders on behalf of our Principals and was paid a commission on such bookings. By this time our staff members had been increased to seven.

At the end of 1974, an Audit Report revealed that the company showed a loss. And it was decided that it was necessary to increase our stock with additional purchases so as to achieve additional sales. In order to do this, I borrowed $25,000.00 from Colonial Life Insurance Company and used my home as Security. At that point our staff members had increased to twelve.

With these additional funds, I decided to make a promotional trip to the United Kingdom, Holland, Denmark, Canada, United States of America, Trinidad and Barbados at a cost of $8,816.00. The trip was very successful, having secured additional agencies. I also made some purchases of food products while on the trip.

In addition to purchasing products from local distributors, we were now, as a result of foreign business procured, importing British American Tobacco products, powdered milk from Denmark, Condensed and Evaporated milk from Holland, canned and pickled meats from Holland and various manufactured products from Trinidad and Barbados.

At the end of our financial year in 1979, Coopers & Lybrand's audited report showed that our net profit was $47,070.00. In the meantime, our staff numbers had significantly increased and also our sales. At the end of the financial year in 1985, our net profit had increased to $217,738.00, and our office, sales department and storeroom were moved to larger premises. During six years of operating from this location, we acquired two sales vans which distributed products in country areas. We secured additional agencies with suppliers in Australia, New Zealand, the United States of America, Canada, Guyana, Columbia and various European countries.

At this juncture, I wish to state that my original plan was that Independence Agencies Limited would be a family business, but due to the shortage of finance, I invited some friends to purchase Shares to increase the Capital. At the end of 1979 there were five other Shareholders in addition to my family.

Due to the relentless expansion of the business, the Empire Cinema building on the Carenage was purchased during the latter part of 1987. The property was renovated and our operations were relocated there in mid-July 1988.

In 1995, we bought a building at Grand Anse which was renovated and enlarged two years later. Our operations there are conducted under the name of C.K's Super Valu Food Depot.

In 2000, we were approached by Goddard Enterprises Limited with an offer to buy the company, if not fully, at least a controlling interest. Goddard's request was discussed at shareholders' meetings and it was decided that we would negotiate to sell 51% of the shares to Goddard if their offer was acceptable. After many meetings with Goddard and after consultations with our Auditors and a Construction & Engineering Consultant Company, we agreed to sell the 51% Shareholding of the company to Goddard Enterprises Limited. The selling price was 26.7 times the original value of the Shares.

The sale was finalised during the latter part of 2001, and it was agreed that I would remain as Managing Director until 31st August 2003, when I should retire, but that my sons Ken Sylvester and Brian Sylvester would remain as Assistant Managing Directors, and that my daughter Yolande Radix, who was also a Director, would remain as Manager of C.K.'s Super Valu Food Depot; and that all staff members, who numbered sixty-five at the time, would continue to be employed by the company. Also, that the company's trading name would remain Independence Agencies Limited and C.K. Super Valu Food Depot, respectively."

THE EMPLOYER

When Independence Agencies Limited was originally set up, the company operated from two rooms on the first floor of a residential property, and there were at the initial stage just three members of staff, including the founder. But as the business developed and expanded, larger premises for stocking merchandise and an increase in staffing numbers were being demanded. Consequently, at the height of Independent Agencies Limited's success, the number of staff employed spiralled to sixty or more.

Although C.K. became a hugely successful businessman, teaching remained his vocation and he would use his past experiences in the education arena to deliver personal training to his staff. And having assumed responsibility for staff recruitment, he personally trained all successful applicants for the specific posts offered.

C.K. managed the professional side of the business with a firm hand and the highest standards were at all times expected.

Sub-standard performances were never acceptable and all workers were required to arrive and be ready to begin their duties at the designated time. But C.K. led by example by at all times practising what he preached. He was the first person to arrive at the office, usually no later than 5.00 am, and the last to leave in the evening. And he was a "hands-on" employer who, on a daily basis, demonstrated commitment by being focused on ensuring that Independence Agencies Limited maintained the reputation of being reliable in expediting a first class service. But the support of an equally focused, effective and efficient team was crucial for achieving the desired outcomes, and required the input of additional working hours in order to meet specific deadlines whenever it became necessary. Although overtime payments were not made, employees were entitled to take time off equivalent to extra hours worked. Most importantly, end-of-year profits were shared with the staff and took the form of large annual bonuses at Christmas.

Susan Skeete who had been a secretary with the company for 17 years, said that in relation to required tasks C.K.'s motto was: "Do it now – Don't put if off". She also recalled a particular incident when errors were identified in a typed document submitted. C.K. allegedly did not conceal his disapproval and with some emphasis advised that, if unsure, she should either ask or use the dictionary. The lesson learnt as a result of the mistake would never be forgotten.

Marsha Newton, a member of the Accounts personnel for over 19 years, reported that C.K. had been an "honest" and "straightforward" boss with high expectations. He would say, if in doubt, ask. Don't carry on in uncertainty. C.K. was always willing to provide assistance but inaccuracies were totally unacceptable.

Loraine Morgan, a secretary with Independence Agencies Limited for more than 32 years, said that C.K. had been a "no nonsense" boss whose motto was: "Do it now. Do it good."

Michael Marshall, a salesman for over 20 years, recalled being on occasions summoned to the Managing Director's office where, in stern tones, he was informed of a specific undertaking that may not have quite met the standard required of the company, but that the difficult sessions would always end on a positive note with the delivery of reassuring and constructive advice on the way forward.

Despite being uncompromising with regard to the company's Policies and Procedures, C.K. never failed to provide positive feedback when appropriate; and individual staff members would receive periodical appraisals on their work progress and performance.

Individual staff members would smile to themselves whenever they heard their employer loudly and victoriously exclaim "There you are!" each time a "searched-for" contact name had been located in the well-thumbed Card Index. No doubt any visitor overhearing the excited tones would have been excused for assuming that C.K. had actually won something very significant such as a jackpot of some kind.

C.K. was alleged to have never used a computer. Nor did he, at the time, employ a book-keeper and was said to have kept on top by storing and evaluating all aspects of the business in his head! When Ken suggested to his father that the company should open a second office in a town at the far end of the island, C.K. replied: "How could you expect me to be in two places at the same time." The response may have been suggestive of a man who had been determined in maintaining full and overall control of his business empire, and delegating appeared not to have been practised. C.K. did not rely on an H.R. Department or a Training Officer. All staff-related issues were among components for the smooth operation of a company that were independently undertaken. And he could, in that case, have been considered an extraordinary one-man co-operative.

FROM HUMBLE BEGINNINGS

The desk used by the Managing Director was alleged to have been covered in a disorganised and chaotic heap of papers, files and documents lying on top of each other or scattered in different directions. Despite this fact, C.K. always appeared to know where everything was placed. Consequently, Marsha Newton was surprised when she entered the boss's office one day and found him in a state of panic and frantically searching.

"Have you lost something?" she asked.

"Yes," was the reply, "can't find my glasses."

"They're on your head!" was the immediate response.

C.K. paused for a second before confirming the observation. And on discovering the misplaced spectacles had been all the while perched on the top of his head, he exclaimed, in surprised tones, "How on earth did they get there!?"

Ken Sylvester described his father as being "stern and firm". "He is a hard nut, but the nut is easy to crack," he said. This statement very much reflected C.K.'s managerial approach. Although he managed his staff with a firm hand, he was, nevertheless, an employer with heart, and, provided his staff performed well, there was never a problem.

C.K. was said to have operated an open-door policy, his office door being at all times open and welcoming, and even though he held the authoritative position of Managing Director, employees were never made to feel intimidated on entering his office. Indeed, the overall environment was relaxed and comfortable. In particular, everyone was welcomed to view popular sporting events on the television that had been installed in his office.

C.K. loved sweets and would invariably have them lying on the side of his desk. Staff members were always invited to help themselves whenever they came into his office. But on realising one day that his favourite variety had been disappearing a little too fast, he uncharacteristically decided to hide them. But when in a quiet moment the time seemed right for indulging undisturbed in his guilty pleasure, he was unable to find the hidden sweets. Needless to say, C.K. had been most disappointed.

C.K. was described as being a "father-figure boss" who tried to make his staff "feel comfortable". He was said to be approachable, a good listener and individuals felt enabled to discuss their personal problems with him. He never failed to offer helpful advice and their confidentiality was always respected. C.K. was overall considered "a caring man" by his employees.

Requests for time off work were never or extremely rarely denied. And C.K. did not hesitate in sponsoring separate loan applications. Michael Marshall said that, after overhearing his angry outburst to a colleague that he had been turned down for a loan, C.K. called him into the office and offered to help. The boss's intervention resulted in the original decision being reversed.

It may have been to some extent a reflection on his own personal life experiences that C.K. advised the young salesman to stay away from alcohol and cigarettes, get married, settle down and do not get divorced; and by so doing avoid being lonely in old age. Michael Marshall said, "He was like a dad to me."

It was undoubtedly because of the personable manner of the man at the top that a warm, friendly and inclusive atmosphere was being generated within the offices of Independent Agencies Limited. It was a place where individuals felt free to interact not only with each other but also the Managing Director on a first name basis. C.K. had been thought of as a "fun person" who enjoyed having a joke and laugh with his staff. He attended their weddings and christenings and was even present at Graduation ceremonies.

Indeed, staff outings organised by C.K. included bus trips, visits to interesting sporting events, luncheons at restaurants of choice or at the office, with individuals bringing a dish from home. Various members of staff would be invited to accompany their Manager to Trade Fairs, where they would be required to test and recommend suitable saleable products for the company. It was further indication that C.K. valued his staff, their contributions and their opinions.

Eric Gairy was, like C.K., one of many young individuals of his era who sought their fortune in a foreign land. But in December 1949, he returned to Grenada from Curacao where he had been a Trade Unionist and in 1950 founded the Grenada Manual, Maritime and Intellectual Workers' Union. Eric Gairy was destined to be the first elected Prime Minister of Grenada, Carriacou and Petite Martinique, following independence.

C.K. had always championed the rights of the working man and supported Gairy and what he stood for. However, on learning that his own employees had put forward an application for union representation and were planning a vote on the nomination of a Shop Steward, C.K. was dismayed. He considered that he had been a fair employer and responded by convening, at short notice, a staff meeting. C.K. confronted his staff and in no uncertain terms asserted that if they became unionised, bonuses would be smaller, and all perks, including compassionate leave, staff outings and the sponsoring of loans, would be terminated with immediate effect. He followed this up by asking for a show of hands of all those intending to join up with a union. None was raised. C.K.'s direct and straightforward deliberations had served to refresh their memories of the benefits they received. Moreover, knowing the character of the man, there could be no questioning that his warnings would be fully carried out. Staff members were long-standing. They had all been employed with the company for a number of years and were embarrassed that they had overlooked or taken as given the benefits they received from a boss who, although strict, was at the same time kind, considerate and inclusive. And they were grateful. Consequently, the issue regarding union representation was never again discussed and the *status quo* remained.

The original intention of Independent Agencies Limited being a family-run concern had long been abandoned because of unforeseen financial difficulties. Nevertheless, C.K.'s all-embracing management style could have been considered reflective of a large family unit. In spite of the rigid policies that had been put into place for ensuring the upkeep of the company's reputable high standards, C.K. had in parallel created a working environment that was relaxed, comfortable, caring and sharing; a fact underlined by workers who said of C.K.: "He was a caring man"; "A father-figure"; "A dad to me"; "A fun person"; "Honest and straightforward"; "A no-nonsense boss"; "Once you do your work good, you would never have a problem with him."

The comments testified that C.K. Sylvester had been an employer who brandished the stick with one hand but offered a carrot with the other; and that the combination of methods never failed in being effective.

DEALINGS WITH CUSTOMERS

Independence Agencies Limited had been the most prominent company on the island with a reputation for delivering a reliably expeditious service. It was indeed the leading wholesale provider of essential commodities on the island. Many companies negotiated purchase contracts by way of written credit agreements which, on the whole, were being adhered to. But there was always the odd customer whose payments for goods ordered were not forthcoming, despite repeated written reminders.

C.K., known to be a principled no-nonsense business operator who would not be bowed, remained resolute that, one way or another, money owed to the company will be paid. And his one-man debt recovery team was always ready and willing to assert unanticipated action, whenever necessary.

In the case of one particular customer who failed to settle his credit despite a series of payment requests, C.K. acted by taking his staff for lunch at a restaurant owned by the particular businessman. They were directed to ignore the price and select whatever they fancied on the menus. After everyone had "pigged out" on their favourite meal, washed down by beverages of choice, the total costs were calculated by a waiter and on C.K.'s request placed on the Credit Account he held with the restaurant.

Staff luncheons were booked at the same eating place on several subsequent occasions and followed the pattern of everyone being encouraged to order their separate menu preferences, with total costs being added to C.K.'s Credit Account. The series of expensive mid-day outings enjoyed by C.K. and his staff ceased when he was satisfied that the overall costs of food consumed equalled the sum of the outstanding credit that was owed to his company. But the owner of the restaurant only became aware that C.K. had recovered the debt by alternative means when the accumulated bill for meals eaten remained unpaid.

In relation to another customer who failed to honour his credit agreement, despite many requests for payment, the One-Man Debt Recovery Team went into action. C.K. fearlessly entered the stables owned by the particular individual and boldly helped himself to one of several well-groomed horses. As far as C.K. was concerned, the horse had been just payment for services delivered that remained unpaid.

The horse was subsequently given the name "Strike Pay", which seemed appropriate under the circumstances. And C.K. hit on the idea of commissioning a Jockey and having his new possession trained for entry into the island's annual horse-racing event.

The day of "The Races" eventually arrived, but no one considered "Strike Pay" a serious contender. But family and friends decided nonetheless to show their support by having a little flutter on C.K.'s horse. And it was not long before the announcement,

"They're off", resounded throughout the racing venue as the race in which "Strike Pay" was competing began. Soon eyes widened and individuals rose to their feet as what was initially considered unlikely, suddenly appeared very much likely when "Strike Pay" was spotted among the front runners. C.K. and his family rose to their feet, cheered excitedly and bellowed, "Come on! Come on!"

The horse was geed all the way to the finishing line and everyone was staggered that it had actually won the race! C.K. immediately sprinted to the enclosure and heartily congratulated both rider and horse. It had been a momentous moment.

THE HELPING HAND

It was said by one employee of Independence Agencies Limited that C.K. would shrug his shoulders and respond with the words, "Everybody have to live", when alerted to competitors who may have stolen his ideas. He was indeed an altruistic soul who wished good for others and would extend a helping hand to the ordinary man. In particular, C.K. had been willing always to offer a helping hand to those who struggled to get a foot on the ladder. In so doing, he provided employment or stood as guarantor on loan applications for a number of individuals who sought his assistance.

One such person was James Lewis, who became acquainted with C.K. when he was employed as a Store Keeper. The young man had for several years been trying to obtain a bank loan for starting a business, but his applications were being repeatedly refused. Essentially, the prospective businessman had no collateral. His background was poor, his education had been elementary and as a consequence he was able only to secure low-paid manual employment. Moreover, he had not been closely acquainted with anyone who was in a financial position to provide the necessary security for obtaining a loan.

With doors being constantly slammed in his face and seemingly no prospects on the horizon, it appeared that all hope had been lost. But at his darkest moment, James Lewis disclosed his experienced difficulties to C.K. The response was unexpectedly encouraging. C.K. actually took the risk of personally taking out the desired loan on behalf of the aspiring entrepreneur and a written easy repayment contract was subsequently agreed upon and signed by both parties. The young man went on to establish Country Cold Store, a highly successful wholesale and retail business with customers throughout Grenada, Carriacou and Petite Martinique.

C.K.'s altruism is being credited for this "rags to riches" tale. He had reached out a helping hand to a man who had experienced only rejection and could find no window of opportunity for turning his business vision into reality. C.K.'s involvement completely changed the lives of one man and his family. They would be forever grateful.

GIVING BACK TO SOCIETY

C.K. did not take for granted the huge profitable annual gains that were being sustained by Independence Agencies Limited and felt the need to repay society. Charitable payments were made to schools, churches, various organisations and also specific individuals where necessary.

Sport had always been one of C.K.'s main interests and even though he was "not good at it", had been dedicated to the development of sport on the island. He sponsored and supported various football, netball, basketball, boxing and cricket clubs; and aspiring sportsmen and women, including young and up-coming cricketers, were also separately sponsored by the company.

Financial donations were made for the development of sporting facilities in both primary and secondary schools across the island. Trophies were donated and cash payments made in support of inter-island tournaments and sporting and cultural activities held in Grenada and Carriacou.

Indeed, C.K. had been a well-known and respected associate of Ministers at the Department of Sport and was regularly invited onto the panel that considered and selected the Sports Personality of the particular year from nominations submitted.

But C.K.'s sporting passion remained the game of cricket and he had travelled to countries including Australia, England, Guyana, Trinidad, Barbados, St. Lucia and St. Kitts to support the West Indies cricket team when they played international Test matches.

The West Indies Cricket Board had been established in the early 1920s and began competing in international matches in 1928. But sixty-four years would elapse before a Grenadian National would be included in the team. Consequently, it was not surprising that almost every person who lived on the islands of Grenada, Carriacou and Petite Martinique, including C.K. Sylvester, was jubilant when in 1992 news broke that one of their own had been selected to play for the West Indies in Australia. The young man was called Junior Murray, a 24-year-old cricketer who resided in a suburb of St George, known as River Road.

Junior Murray's unprecedented sporting accomplishment motivated C.K. into making sure that the now professional cricketer was suitably rewarded for his remarkable achievement. He acted by organising a collection involving better-off members of the community, well-wishers, friends and other interested persons. C.K. made his own contribution to the pot before obtaining a Bank cheque for the total amount.

But C.K. had no intention of missing his countryman's first game at international level. He reserved an airline ticket to Australia and booked into the very hotel in which the West Indies Cricket Team had booked to stay. C.K. arrived in Australia on Christmas

Eve of 1992 and on Christmas Day delivered a cheque to Junior Murray for $2500.00.

As a representative of Grenada, C.K. was treated as a special guest and seated at the Official Stand alongside other respected dignitaries at the first Test match in Melbourne on Boxing Day 1992. But Junior Murray had not been picked to play. C.K. then followed the team to Sidney, where the second Test was scheduled to be played on New Year's Day 1993, and was delighted to find that Junior had been included in the team. C.K. became one of a very few Grenadians who had been privileged to see the first Grenadian cricketer play at international level. He would on a subsequent occasion travel to Manchester, England, to watch Junior Murray play for the West Indies in a test match against the host nation. It had been a worthwhile trip. The West Indies won the series and C.K. was joyful.

ACCOLADES

As a 12-year-old boy, the winning of a Scholarship for entry into the prestigious Grenada Boys' Secondary School had been for C.K. the best of all accolades.

But as an adult, C.K. may have been unable to imagine a sporting accolade that could surpass the selection of his fellow countryman, Junior Murray, in the West Indies Cricket Team. The nation as a whole shared the feeling that they had received some kind of award. Moreover, C.K. may have derived personal satisfaction and a sense of gratitude that his life-long enthusiasm and support of the game had at last paid dividends.

C.K. felt honoured and humbled when he was unexpectedly notified in June 1995 that he had been awarded an MBE from Her Majesty the Queen in recognition of many years of sustained assistance to the development of sport in general on the islands of Grenada, Carriacou and Petite Martinique.

The various successes of individuals as a result of C.K.'s support and assistance had, albeit on a personal level, also been satisfyingly rewarding. He was in particular extremely proud of Julius Isaac, a school friend to whom private tuition was delivered at a fee of just one shilling each month. The ambitious young Julius went on to study Law abroad and progressed to being the highest Judge in Canada. No other black man had previously attained the acclaimed position. It was, to C.K., quite unbelievable. The idea that he may have contributed to his friend's exceptional attainment had been staggering. It was for C.K. very much a personal accolade.

Although C.K. did not have the benefit of a father-figure on whom his own parenting methods could be modelled, he nonetheless endeavoured to be a reliably responsible father to his own offspring. It followed that one of his most appreciated personal accolades was that his children had all grown up to be hard-working, high-achieving and respected members of society, and between them had provided him with nine grandchildren and six great-grandchildren.

The phenomenal success of his company, Independence Agencies Limited, carried along by the support of a cohesive, loyal and long-serving team of workers, was also among C.K. Sylvester's greatest accolades.

RETIREMENT

In the year 2000 an offer to purchase Independent Agencies Limited was forwarded. It resulted in a series of meetings and consultations with shareholders, the prospective purchasers and the Company Auditors. It was finally agreed subject to specific conditions to sell 51% of the shareholdings.

A significant condition attached to the sale stipulated that the staff structure and designated personnel would remain. In particular, C.K. would continue in his role as Managing Director until his retirement on 31st August 2003.

All too soon the date of retirement arrived. A party to commemorate the special occasion had been for some time in preparation and everyone involved looked forward to the retirement celebrations with anticipation tinged with much sadness. It was hard to imagine that the man who had been the consistent face of authority at the office for so many years would suddenly no longer be there.

But C.K. had been well aware that nothing lasts forever and that the longest road will eventually reach its end. He had been working continually for a total of sixty-two years, including thirty years as the Managing Director of the company he founded, Independent Agencies Limited. The time had come for him to hand over the reins to his heir and step back into a well-earned and deserved life of leisure.

C.K.'s usual attire was smart but fashionably casual, with ties being worn only at particular events such as weddings and funerals. His retirement party on 31st August 2003 had been for C.K. one of the rare occasions that warranted the donning of a tie, but it would be large, colourful and prominently eye-catching. And as he fixed it into place, C.K. may have cast his mind back to the very first time he wore a tie. He was at the time just 12 years old and in his new school uniform when, for a short while, he felt himself being transformed into a person of importance. C.K. never imagined that the brief moments of fantasy would one day become a reality.

Everyone present at C.K.'s retirement celebration for a moment held their breath as he strolled into the venue. They had never before seen him look so handsome or more smartly attired; but with his flashy tie, C.K. had succeeded in being, as always, smart but casual. Within minutes of arrival, cheers and loud applause echoed across the venue and it was not long before the party was in full swing. And while the band played, the environment buzzed as drinks flowed and food was served and consumed with relish.

The pivotal moments during the celebration demanded silence as individuals in turn spoke about their positive experiences with the retiree and how much he would be missed. Speeches were followed by everyone raising glasses of champagne and giving a toast to C.K. They wished him long life and continued good health. And C.K. welled up with emotion on hearing the beautiful tune composed by staff members, in honour of his retirement, being melodically strummed on steel drums, at the end of what had been considered a most memorable occasion.

PHOTO GALLERY

Marriage Register

Vernice Sylvia Banfield

and

Cecil Kenrick Sylvester

were united in Holy Matrimony on *Saturday*

the *30th* day of *October 1948*

at *Roxborough R. C. Church*

St. Paul's

Grenada B.W.I.

Marriage Register

CK and Vernice Sylvester - Wedding Party Photo

L – R First daughter(Cutie), first wife(Vernice), first vehicle(Ford)

First CK Family L – R Vernice, Cutie, Ken, Cecily and CK

Vernice Sylvia Banfield Sylvester – She Is Royal!!

Vernice admiring flowers or flowers admiring Vernice?

L – R Cecily, Kenrick, Cutie

CK and his extended family celebrate his 88th birthday. Back row, left to right, C.K., grandson Ryan, son Ken, Ken's wife Lois and extended relatives. Front row, Brendon Batson, wife Cecily, Cutie with her husband Peter Radix.

CK a prolific sponsor of soccer, cricket, netball, basketball and karate poses with his daughter Cutie in front of the FIFA World Cup Trophy

CK Sylvester The Man

Yolande 'Cutie' Radix – Executive Publisher

C.K. accompanies choir on visit to Pennsylvania

Jean Bovell

MOVING ON AFTER RETIREMENT

Ken Sylvester said that his father had many acquaintances but no close friends, an observation that was most apparent following his retirement. C.K.'s second marriage which took place in 1968 ended in divorce during the year 1994. But despite the absence of a close companion with whom he could share his later years, C.K. would ease into a relaxed and enjoyable chapter in his life. Indeed, it was not too long before C.K. adjusted into his retirement and transferred his main purpose from work to leisure. But having been always a disciplined individual, C.K. needed structure in his life and applied it to his day-to-day routines. He would begin each day with an early-morning swim in the ocean and would afterwards pursue the scheduled activity of interest.

C.K. had been cruising along happily in retirement when out of the blue, during the early months of 2009, the family received news that second daughter and sister, Cecily, who had been residing in England with her husband and family, was diagnosed with having a stage 4 brain tumour. The family was shocked and devastated. In particular, C.K. could not believe that his "little girl" had been struck by such a savage illness. He was inconsolable, but strengthened by his Faith. Always a staunch Catholic, C.K. in retirement had been devoting more time to his religion, which would prove a great comfort during the ensuing difficult months.

Although family and friends hoped and prayed for a miracle, Cecily would eventually succumb to her illness. She passed peacefully in bed with a "smile" on her face at the family home in England, surrounded by close family members including sister Cutie, on 18th September 2009. She was 58 years of age. Cecily's ashes were subsequently taken to the land of her birth and placed in the grave of her mother. It had been an emotionally challenging period for C.K. and the rest of the family.

Time moved on and C.K. continued to keep himself busy while trying to come to terms and learning to live with the persistent pain of losing one of his beloved daughters.

C.K. had been a man of leisure for almost ten years when his landmark 90th birthday was celebrated with much cheer and rejoicing. C.K. could not have been happier that he had actually crossed the significant milestone. He considered himself a very lucky man to have lived so long.

Despite maintaining robust physical health and a sharp memory, C.K.'s mobility began to slow down when he reached the approximate age of 92. It was also a period when his sense of hearing began to deteriorate. Now in his twilight years, C.K. spends the majority of his time relaxing quietly at the home he shares with younger son Brian and his family, but looks forward to being on a regular basis taken on rides to places of interest by his daughter, Cutie.

C.K. is grateful to have been blessed with a long and eventful life. His aspirations and goals had been achieved to the fullest. C.K. admits to no regrets and considers that his life has been "a most pleasant one".

EPILOGUE

Born into abject poverty, C.K. Sylvester was raised by a single and unsupported mother who was resolute that her son should have a better life, and who ensured that he received the best education available, which she believed was the key to opening the door to future prosperity. But although Albertha had achieved the desired educational goal, C.K. would enter the world of work with no particular direction or career objective in mind. He simply searched for work and would have been happy and willing to take any job offered.

And so it was that C.K. Sylvester abandoned himself to the torrents of life and simply went with the flow. But his confidence had been boosted by his educational attainments and he tackled the waves with determination and drive. Indeed, C.K. rose to the challenges that were presented in every position held and has been appropriately rewarded for his productive efforts. He had no idea that he was being steered on a path that would lead to his true calling. The discovery led to the achievement of a prosperous life. It had been the long-term goal that Albertha desired for her son.

C.K. went on to become a highly respected and admired member of society whose charitable contributions were recognised and honoured. He had also been considered a "father-figure" by those to whom he offered a listening ear, provided helpful advice or lent a helping hand.

Some might say that C.K. Sylvester's rise from poverty to prosperity had been pre-determined by fate and that he simply played the hand he was dealt. Others might put it down to coincidence or that he was "just lucky".

Whether or not C.K.'s life journey had been guided by divine order or had simply been a series of coincidences, there can be no denying the fact that he was an innately principled individual with an abundance of self-belief and perseverance, who was driven by the need to succeed. In conclusion, Cecil Kenrick Sylvester MBE accomplished success by being charismatic, passionately hardworking, and ensuring, with the support of a valued team of enthusiastic workers, that Independence Agencies Limited maintained the delivery of a first class service.

The End

www.ingramcontent.com/pod-product-compliance
Lightning Source LLC
Chambersburg PA
CBHW070952080526
44587CB00015B/2273